Designs *of* Omission

America's Original Sin

harrington
young, inc.

harringtonyoung@icloud.com
harringtonyoung.com

ISBN 979-8-9860239-0-8

This book has been has been typeset with Adobe Caslon Pro, based upon the original font designed by William Caslon I (c. 1692–1766) in London. Benjamin Franklin used it extensively. It was the font used to set both the Declaration of Independence and the U.S. Constitution.*

Cover art: U.S. Constitution © National Archives, archives.gov
Equality Equity graphic © Angus Maguire,
Interaction Institute for Social Change

Cover design by Jilian Aesir, Harrington Young
Book design and production by Harrington Young

With admiration, gratitude, and hope
for Shizue, Nobuko, Reiko, and Ron

Also by Byron Noriyoshi Kunisawa

BOOKS & PUBLICATIONS
I Made It
From Me to We: A Hierarchy of Multicultural Concepts
A Guide to Multicultural Drug Abuse Prevention
A Nation in Crisis: The Dropout Dilemma
Diversity Management: The Key to NWS Continued Success
Co-author, Workforce Diversity: Linking Diversity to Quality
Sports columnist, Kick Off Magazine

VIDEOS
Work for Diversity: Opportunities for the 21st Century
Transportation Conference Workforce Diversity:
Opportunities for the 21st Century
Institutional Designs of Omission
Our Multicultural Nation, a lecture series

ORGANIZATIONS
Co-founder, Multicultural Training Resource Center, San Francisco
Co-founder, California State Multicultural Aids Prevention Center,
San Francisco
Co-founder, National Multicultural Drug Prevention Committee
National Institute on Drug Abuse,
National Institute on Drug Prevention,
Rockville, Maryland

Designs *of* Omission

America's Original Sin

Dale —
Thank you!!
Byron

Byron Noriyoshi Kunisawa

**harrington
young, inc.**

Table of Contents

EQUALITY

EQUITY

These images are provided courtesy of Interaction Institute for Social Change, who engaged artist Angus Maguire to show the difference between Equality and Equity. The image below illustrates the effect of the removal of institutional and systemic barriers, resulting in access and, for this book, representing Inclusion.

INCLUSION

Glossary of Terms

culture is a complex and rich concept defined by a community or society. It structures the way people view the world. It involves a particular set of beliefs, norms, and values concerning the nature of relationships, the way people live their lives, and how they organize their environments.

democracy is used in the colloquial sense to describe American government and society, although technically a democratic republic.

design of omission is any document, plan, regulation, law, or construct which consciously or unwittingly affects the exclusion of an individual or group, effectively precluding them for perpetuity.

inclusion is the process of improving the scope of participation for people who are disadvantaged. It is both a process and a goal. The issues of inclusion and exclusion are multidimensional, relational, and dynamic along a continuum between the two states.

ethnicity refers to the social identity and mutual belongingness that defines a group of people based on common origins, shared beliefs, and shared standards of behavior (culture).

equality is the state of being equal in terms of status, rights and opportunities. Equality means each individual or group accesses the same resources or opportunities.

equity is the quality of being fair and impartial. Equity recognizes that each person has different circumstances and allocates the exact resources and opportunities needed to reach an equal outcome.

exclusion is a product of omission, a state in which individuals are unable to participate fully in economic, social, political and cultural life. Exclusion is both an outcome and a process resulting from lack of access to material resources including income, employment, land and housing, and to services such as education and health care. Exclusion entails not only material deprivation but also lack of agency or control over important decisions as well as feelings of alienation and inferiority. In nearly all countries, age, sex, disability, race, ethnicity, religion, migration status, socioeconomic status, place of residence, sexual orientation and gender identity have been grounds for exclusion.

xi

institutional racism refers to the policies, practices, and norms that incidentally but inevitably perpetuate inequality, resulting in significant economic, legal, political and social restrictions.

Issei, Nisei, Sansei are first generation immigrants from Japan, second generation born in America, and third generation, many born in internment camps in America.

Latinx represents all descending cultures and ethnicities from Spain and Portugal, including Chicano, Hispanic, Latino, Mexican, Central and South American.

original sin is a secular literary metaphor used in *Designs of Omission* theory to represent the legal omission of enslaved Blacks, Indigenous peoples, and women from The Constitution.

race is a social construct that describes people with shared physical characteristics, and is associated with caste or class.

racism is an attitude or belief that people with specific shared physical features are superior or inferior to others.

Foreword

Designs of Omission, America's Original Sin should be proclaimed a national treasure. It should be included as part of a canon of literary and scholarly works around which a mandatory orientation process for every elected and appointed office of public power ought to be developed. Kunisawa has produced a readable journey through twenty-six generations of American history that every reader can digest. He lets the truth speak for itself, which has its own power to transform minds and hearts.

Eighteen generations had passed from 1500, when the first Europeans arrived on the continent they would call "America," (omitting "White") to 1860, when the former British citizens segregated themselves as they geared up for a civil war that would determine the fate of Black people, and other nonwhite populations, in an onerous economic system steeped in human trafficking and constructed for the benefit of a Whites-only national citizenry. A White nation that was born on a continent with more than 500 existing nations of indigenous peoples and characterized each state joining the new Union by either "slave-owning" or "slave-free" has struggled mightily to hide the truth, which lives in plain sight: The United States of White America began in 1776 ironically with a Declaration of Independence recognizing that "all men are created equal" while a majority of the nation's founders were slaveowners along with a majority of its thirteen states (eight) which were established on lands that White Americans obtained by killing the nonwhite people who lived on them for more than a millennium. Kunisawa doesn't brush past this truth nor diminish it. It is at the center of the struggle that plagues today's generations.

From the U.S. Civil War in 1861, to the ousting of another White supremacist president in 2020, eight generations of White Americans struggled violently over the question of how (or whether) to redesign, reform and reconstruct White America into a more Inclusive America with equitable ownership of the American Dream of prosperity.

The struggle of White Americans over the last eight generations to include, integrate, value and empower nonwhite populations in "their country" is a story that has been carefully crafted and controlled by the conquering White supremacists, who lost the Civil War but won the political and economic battles that enabled them to tell their own version of brand America. The supremacist ideal of America is a narrative of the most benevolent, meritocratic, greatest nation the world has ever seen, which has permeated every nook and cranny of American society. *Designs of Omissions* exposes the fallacies and falsehoods of the supremacist narrative.

Kunisawa elevates an understanding of the equal value in all humanity while exposing the systems steeped in racial hierarchy (valuing/devaluing humans by race), which is at the core of the story of how America was born and evolved. Throughout the last three generations, particularly, the supremacist narrative of America has been challenged in extraordinary ways. Through the undeniable reality of nonviolent direct-action protests rising up in nearly 1,000 cities in 1963, led by Dr. Martin Luther King Jr and other prominent Black men and women, and supported by thousands of White allies at every socioeconomic level, the truth of the "shameful condition" White America created for its Black citizenry which King described in his most iconic speech, has seeped to the surface of America's national debate and racial discord. Myriad voices offer irrefutable evidence while crying out in chronic pain to a majority of White Americans whose minds have been conditioned to ignore, dismiss or deny the outcry by generations of mythology and propaganda promulgated by trusted institutions: family, schools, universities, churches, media, business leaders and policymakers. Kunisawa's voice figures prominently in that chorus crying out for the attention of today's generations.

In *Designs of Omission*, Kunisawa reminds us that despite the distortions of truth and omissions of contextual facts (and peoples) throughout history, the truth has continued like a steady drumbeat to rise above the noise that seeks to drown it out and prevent it from reaching the ears, heart and soul of this nation. New generations provide new opportunities to build a common ground of understanding and collective action.

From W.E.B. Du Bois' *Black Reconstruction in America 1860-1880*, which describes in scholarly detail the truth about the Civil War and generational efforts to change laws, systems, policies and practices that would shape and mold the society we inherited today, to Dr. Martin Luther King Jr.'s *Why We Can't Wait*, which describes the rise of a "Negro Revolution" that became what the federal government called "the most important movement in American history" (and continues to this day), there are few books that reveal so many deeply held secrets of this White America. *Designs of Omission* inspires and empowers the reader to become empathetic societal change agents.

Kunisawa establishes in *Designs of Omission* a foundation of new knowledge for generations today that can build a common ground of understanding across racial divides which can lead to productive dialogue and perhaps collective collaboration to resume the work of the White and Black "Radicals" following the Civil War and the nonviolent "Revolutionaries" of the 1960s, whose dreams of a "beloved community" can only be achieved when generations of Americans of all races agree on a common vision of equitable access and outcomes for a 21st century multicultural America.

This book offers its readers a paradigm-shifting lens of historical context that envisions an Inclusive America for future generations, which can only be realized if generations alive today will accept one undeniable truth: For an Inclusive America to live, White supremacy must die. ***Designs of Omission*** inspires us to accept that truth and work toward achieving the dream of an inclusive society.

— *Mike Green*

Mike Green is a Cultural Economist, Co-founder of Common Ground Conversations on Race in America, and Chief Strategist at the National Institute for Inclusive Competitiveness, Consultant, Speaker, Author.

Preface

I am *Sansei,* a third-generation Japanese American who learned about exclusion in the 4th grade. Our teacher instructed us to place a colored pin on the city we were born in on a full United States wall map. During my turn, I went to the map but could not find my birth city. After what seemed an eternity, my teacher offered to help me and asked where I was born. "Topaz, Utah," I replied as she proceeded to search, also unable to locate the city.

She announced there was no such place and to ask my mother where I was born. When my mom returned from work, I asked where I was born. She furrowed her brow and replied sarcastically, you are in the 4th grade, and you don't know where you were born? "I thought I was born in Topaz, Utah, but could not find it on the map." She laughed and said, you could not locate Topaz because it was one of the Internment Camps the Japanese were sent to during World War II. *Internment Camp or Summer Camp, how could they be that dissimilar?*

After reporting to my teacher the next day of my birth in an Internment Camp, she became earnest and stated, "there were no Internment Camps," then instructed me to look in the U.S. History book and prove it existed. However, after checking out three U.S. History books from the library, not one mentioned the existence of the Internment Camps.

My mother provided me with the birth certificate stating place of birth Topaz, Utah. That day at school became a huge problem. When presented with the birth certificate, my teacher still refused to believe the location existed. It was a confusing moment for a 9-year-old, but an epiphany for me. This cognitive dissonance was my first experience with "Designs of Omission."

I began to wonder about the truth and validity of everything I was learning at school. The experience of over 120,000 Japanese Americans had been excluded from the U.S. History books. I was too young to analyze the dilemma, but it was forever embedded in my brain. Years later, I would decipher this exclusion of Japanese Americans, fueled by my desire to see who and what else was excluded from my U.S. History books.

*　*　*　*　*

I have personally learned the benefit of interacting with culturally different individuals in my life experiences. My family was released from internment at Topaz, Utah, in March 1946 and relocated to the west coast in Richmond, California. Since the Japanese had no homes to return to, we were assigned to a Japanese Housing Project. We were then transferred from the Richmond Japanese Housing Project to an African American Housing Project in West Oakland, California. This move was the stepping stone to my cultural diversity learning process.

We were the only Asian family in the project. Mrs. Washington was the first resident to welcome my mom and our family. Her son Earl became my best friend. I did not realize it at the time, but I fit in better in Oakland than with my Japanese neighbors in Richmond. First of all, my mom was a single parent. Most of the Black housing project families were single-parent households, so I felt normal and accepted.

Mrs. Washington was a well-respected matriarch and her unconditional acceptance of our family provided us with instant credibility. Earl and his friends thought it was strange that they had to remove their shoes to enter our home, even though Mrs. Washington had prepared them to expect different customs. Being savvy about differing cultures, my mom realized that Japanese traditions in a non-Japanese environment required change to fit in with a new cultural group. We stopped taking our shoes off to enter our home.

As the youngest of four siblings, it was easier for me to adapt to the new challenges of being in an African American community. Since the African American culture in this project was very verbal and colorful in its conversations and communications, it provided an opportunity for me to come out of my shy and introverted self. I was never treated like an outsider, so was unaware of how I was viewed and judged outside of the housing project. I began to understand the distinction more concretely when the police stopped my friends and me. I was treated differently from my Black friends. The police asked if I were okay and whether those Black kids were bothering me.

I was curious why my friends and their families got dressed up and were so happy to go to church on Sundays. Earl finally invited me one Sunday, and my mom encouraged me to go and "learn something." I was Buddhist, and this was the first Christian church I had ever attended. I was blown away by the experience. Everyone was dressed up, including elaborate headwear, and after the pastor delivered his greeting and sermon, the music and singing began. I soon realized why they were so excited to go to church because after all the inspiring singing and sermons, there was an array of southern fried chicken, collard greens, biscuits, macaroni and cheese, and sweet potato pie for dessert.

When I returned home, my mom was eager to hear what the experience was like for me and what I had learned. Having to think about all that had happened and how much I enjoyed the experience made me realize that I never felt out of place. Everyone was welcoming and made sure I tried all of the food recipes they brought to the church. It would be impossible for me to attempt to capture in writing the depth of the experiences and things that I learned from such a gracious and generous community of African Americans. I always felt safe and included by all my friends and their families. It was my first real experience of inclusion, without any adverse reactions to my racial and ethnic differences. It was a lesson in acceptance and being judged as an individual.

Tough lessons began in elementary school. Other than myself and a few white students, the balance of children were African American. My teachers had experienced a limited pattern of Asian students being quiet, studious, well-prepared, non-verbal, and academically proficient. Then I showed up. I was nothing like their stereotype of Asian students because I was "normal" like my Black friends and students, being gregarious, exceptionally verbal, and somewhat animated. These behaviors immediately translated to an academic assessment of "deficient in capabilities," along with a reassignment to a Special Education Program for slow students.

My new teacher quickly determined that I was not a slow learner. I will never forget the day I saw her laugh so hard she had tears. The incentive in early special programs was a crude behavior modification tool of rewarding success with candy. Not a slow learner, I began amassing so many M&Ms that I would bag and sell them on the playground at recess. This was what my new teacher found so amusing.

Within the month, I was transferred to a Special Education Class called MGM, for Mentally Gifted Minors. The only memorable result of this new classification was the number of field trips. A particularly dull field trip was to the San Francisco Symphony. The music was so boring while we all waited for the drummer to start drumming. I later learned these trips were considered "cultural enhancement events," attempts to provide culturally-deprived groups with European culture, all part of a stringent assimilation process to convert to being American.

I was too young to recognize the institutional racism of having been imprisoned in the internment camp, transferred to housing projects of Japanese, then African Americans, before eventually attending integrated schools in Berkeley. I was also unaware of the institutional racism in the education system and the conscious or unconscious biases of the teachers toward minority individuals resulting in arbitrary placements in and out of Special Education groups. My experiences in the project in Oakland illustrate the allure of a community ethnically and culturally different from me, whom I aspired to enculturate.

*　*　*　*　*

As a *Sansei* Japanese American, I sometimes share personal experiences to diffuse hostility or resistance in others so they may consider and learn from other points of view and experiences. To establish a safe environment devoid of blame, guilt, or defensiveness, I downplay the anger and loss of human dignity, property, and the illegal internment of 120,000 Japanese Americans during World War II. My goal is always to free up discussion, but also to ensure that this will never happen again to any group of citizens in America.

I believe that *participative learning* is paramount to comprehending systemic racism and its impact on African Americans and other people of color. Academic education rarely succeeds in reaching people emotionally, thus not enabling individuals to empathize and internalize the horror and atrocity of racism.

I was able to identify with a young child's frustration and the indelible experience of Jim Crow laws in the American South from the Langston Hughes poem "Merry-go-Round" in 1942.[1]

> Where is the Jim Crow section on this
>   Merry Go Round,
> Mister, cause I want to ride? Down South where
> I come from white and colored can't sit side
> by side. Down South on the train there's a Jim
> Crow car. On the bus we're put in the back—
> But there ain't no back to a Merry-Go-Round!
> Where's the horse for a kid that's Black?

Education is always most successful when it engages its participants. As a public school teacher in Palo Alto, California, my measure of success in a lesson was the number of questions and opinions my students would raise. Sometimes, I would promote discussion by presenting accurate but unfair situations that generated personal opinions regarding equity and the importance of having a voice for dissent. *What is the price for confronting injustice and the price for ignoring it?*

My students, like most of Palo Alto, were predominantly white. We created a comparative lesson on bias toward music by race, generation, and circumstance, where we compared the music of their parents and student peers with that of African Americans. Since my students were not familiar with jazz or soul music, I brought in examples for them. After listening intently to the music, I was amazed that a couple of my students concluded they then understood the difference between being treated like a "group instead of an individual." They had listened to and loved the words of Sly Stone, an African American musician, singer, and songwriter, "don't hate the Blacks, don't hate the whites, if you get bit, just hate the bite." They proudly asked, did we get it? I was impressed by their quick analysis and conclusion. Children can learn and comprehend complex issues and situational history remarkably early in their lives.

My 12-year-old students deciphered the complexity of exclusion and inclusion through the lyrics of Soul Music. How many times have we missed the opportunity, as adults, to discuss and learn about individual experiences and perspectives from white and Black individuals? For example, white individuals, often men, are pilloried for making comments such as "I am not a racist because some of my good friends are Black," or saying to a Black male "you are not like other Blacks." We miss these first-person learning opportunities because we are quick to condemn the motives or fear repercussions from such statements. We need to embrace the openness of white individuals and encourage discussion of exclusion, inclusion, and racism without confrontation and accusation. It is a learning opportunity. We need to explore "why are these particular Black individuals acceptable to you for friendship?" "If your friend is not like other Blacks, then what are other Blacks like?"

Blacks who are your friends and family have a lot more in common with you than race and color of skin. You see each other as individuals, rather than as members of a group. The essence of inclusion is seeing and judging members of a different group as an individual, a positive engagement and an important learning opportunity. Teaching and learning opportunities abound. We have only to recognize and explore them.

During my diversity consulting and public speaking career I learned that disarming anger, fear, and hatred is critical to establishing a haven for learning different points of view and experiences without judgment. Safe spaces are especially useful when having to present difficult concepts such as racism to mixed audiences so they can comprehend the concept and perhaps even identify with a situation.

Winston Churchill proclaimed, "tact is the ability to tell someone to go to hell in such a way that they look forward to the trip." [2] It made me consider that replacing tact with humor might yield the same result. Of course, there is always a fine line between humor and patronage.

I have always attempted to use humor to alleviate hatred and misunderstood beliefs of discrimination and exclusion. Mocking oneself is typically a safe way to introduce levity as a vehicle to discuss delicate and potentially divisive issues. It enables others to identify with a concept, an event, or a reaction. Some measure of levity can highlight critical points and events to stimulate discussion and make a subject more relatable, especially for younger generations.

A running joke in the world is: what do you call someone with the linguistic capability of two languages? *Bilingual.* What do you call someone with the linguistic capability of three languages? *Trilingual.* What do you call someone with the linguistic capability of only one language? *American.*

I am not advocating for jokes about serious matters, but for the employment of levity to weaken walls of resistance to critical acceptance of the reality for others unlike one's self. Levity is a powerful tool in the conveyance of important concepts. A symbolic example of American diversity is our 4th of July Independence Day BBQ. We love to have barbecues with chicken, ribs, burgers, and hot dogs. Families invite their friends and relatives to their celebratory gathering. Imagine that some of those guests invite their friends to your barbecue. Since you do not know their guests, you are caught off guard when you are told, "oh, they are vegetarians," your first reaction being, "why would a vegetarian come to a barbecue?" You consider your vegetarian menu, because there are salads and corn on the cob and multiple dessert options. Then another guest informs you that one of their friends is Jewish and can eat only kosher food. If you ask, "what is kosher food?" you can be assured you do not have any. In a nutshell, this is what it is like to live in America: many uninvited guests showing up with unique customs, culinary diets, and non-English languages, all welcomed by our supreme host, the Lady of Liberty.

We have much more in common with each other than we have differences. Every ethnic culture in America has its "it is what it is" adage, that universal acceptance of injustice beyond one's ability to control, along with the human imperative to prevail. The Japanese say *Shikata ga nai*, "It cannot be helped." The Jewish say *Oy, azoy gait es*, "That's how it goes." The French say *C'est comme ça*, "That's how it is." The Chinese say *Chi ku nai lao*, which translates to a harsh "swallow pain and suffering, and endure hardships."

As we focus on the richness of multiculturalism in America today, it is vital to remember that our distinct ethnicities have more in common with each other, sharing similar cultural beliefs and mores, than any single ethnicity has in common with the Anglo monoculture of our Founders. We must work together and support each other in our common battle against white supremacy and systemic racism which is endemic even in the waning image of a white America.

* * * * *

In 1977, after years of coping with pain and confusion, my older brother, Ron Kunisawa, was diagnosed with kidney failure. His struggles worsened when he had to endure dialysis for six hours, three times a week; we decided to seek a kidney transplant.

We were told it could take years waiting for a donor, also that a family member would be the most likely match for a successful operation. My older sister, Nobu, volunteered first for a testing match, which proved unsuccessful. I was next, and *bingo*, a sufficient match to donate a kidney.

After all the tests were screened and I was approved for the donation, there was a final interview with a doctor to set up the procedure for the transplant at the University of California at San Francisco Hospital, (UCSF). During this interview, the doctor asked me several questions to determine whether I had been coerced to volunteer, and ensure I was aware of the procedures and potential consequences. When I confirmed my willingness to provide the kidney, he said there was a mandatory two-week delay to ensure I wouldn't have second thoughts on the procedure. I explained to him that my brother had been suffering for over two years and was not doing well on dialysis. I did not want to delay; would not change my mind and would sign all release forms at that time. The conversation became contentious, such that another doctor entered the room to inquire what was wrong.

The admittance doctor explained the circumstances to the new physician, who began to engage me, asking critical questions: "Are you Japanese, and is Ron the eldest son in your family?" I answered yes to both. He then asked, "do you and your entire family want this surgery to proceed?" I said "Yes, my whole family, especially I, want this transplant surgery and do not understand the need to put my brother through two more weeks of distress for a response that will not change." The new doctor thought for a few moments, then responded, "we can do this tomorrow if you like." I said, "whoa, how about in two days?" We both laughed, and he quietly left after telling the admittance doctor to proceed with my request.

After the interaction, I asked the admittance doctor if it were true that we could perform the surgery in two days and who was the decision-making doctor. He replied, that was Dr. Oscar Salvatierra, and yes, he can make that decision because he is the Chief of Renal Transplant Services at UCSF. I later learned that Dr. Salvatierra was from Argentina. The important point is that Dr. Salvatierra considered Japanese cultural norms and values and understood how they could play out in a family decision for such a serious undertaking. His diversity literacy comprehension enabled him to decide to override a non-cultural hospital policy for my family.

Although not hired based on this added capability, his cultural background and essential position at the hospital saved my brother's life. I learned early on why all his patients were happy and excited when Dr. Salvatierra made his daily rounds to check on them. I remember asking him how many transplants were successful; he responded that 44 were still living successfully. "Only 44?" He laughed and announced, "we have only performed 44 surgeries since I arrived in 1974."

Dr. Salvatierra informed me that he would be the one to remove my kidney during the transplant and not to worry. On the day of the transplant, I remember my countdown from 100 to 0, under anesthesia, hearing country & western music, and thinking, "oh no, I have died and gone to hell." Apparently, Dr. Salvatierra often performed his surgeries accompanied by country & western music.

He is an amazing man and doctor, and a stellar example of diversity in the ranks of employment with the freedom to exercise his expertise. This story is a personal illustration of diversity being an added value, and the crucial benefits cultural competence can provide.

— *B.K.*

Introduction

I shall be telling this with a sigh
Somewhere ages and ages hence:
Two roads diverged in a wood, and I—
I took the one less traveled by,
And that has made all the difference.
— Robert Frost

*W*e are at a crossroads, once again. Eliott C. McLaughlin wrote, "America rises up regularly. It's in the DNA of a country founded in dissent. Millions have forged their anger into action, from the tax revolts of the nation's earliest days, to the labor, housing, and busing protests that helped shape the Civil Rights movement. The Me Too movement fueled women's marches in 2017 and 2018, and the March for Our Lives demonstrations, born of the Parkland school shooting, each drew in seven-figure attendance." [1]

The Black Lives Matter movement, founded in 2013 to address the steady flow of unarmed Black deaths at the hands of police, was propelled onto the national stage after the 2020 murder of George Floyd in Minneapolis, Minnesota. Police officer Derek Chauvin placed his knee on Mr. Floyd's neck for 9 minutes and 29 seconds, despite cries for his mother and *"I can't breathe,"* which ended in death by asphyxiation. [2] Floyd's murder was filmed, and protests erupted across the globe because nothing was done. Much like "there is no Topaz, Utah," these protests were calls for the recognition of injustices, omissions, and outcries for systemic reform to stop them from recurring.

America triumphed with a victorious revolution from the British, but has floundered in its unsuccessful battle from ethnocentrism to multiculturalism. America is not alone in the quest for equity and justice for its citizens and immigrants. We are one of the most culturally diverse nations in the world, purportedly its greatest democracy; yet we are a living contradiction. America is a racist society despite the growth of its minority populations, which will soon outnumber its original white majority. Racism is inherent in our country's structure, incapable of adapting to an evolving populace because established institutional racism begets systems that ultimately perpetuate it.

Author Ta Nehisi Coates warns us in *The Case for Reparations* that "To ignore the fact that one of the oldest republics in the world was erected on a foundation of white supremacy, to pretend that the problems of a dual society are the same as the problems of unregulated capitalism, is to cover the sin of national plunder with the sin of national lying."[3]

When the majority population ignores the inequities and suffering of its minority populations while simultaneously ensuring that those minority populations remain powerless to change the systems and institutions, those inequities persist. Historically, this process is interrupted only when disenfranchised groups protest and bring attention to discrepancies in the laws and policies of a nation. These voices need to be heard as legitimate cries for change.

America's reaction to the Coronavirus Pandemic illustrated our deviation from traditional societal norms by refusing to simply wear a mask to contain the spread of the deadly disease. Every country in the world that has successfully controlled the spread of the Pandemic has prioritized group norms; *the group is more important than the individual.* The call for universal adherence to wearing masks, social distancing, minimizing group gatherings, testing, and social tracing, are accepted and performed for the good of one's country.

America failed to control the spread of the Pandemic because we did not have a culture believing that the group is more important than the individual. Some refused to wear masks as a statement of individual rights or as an act of political defiance.

In August 1976 writer Tom Wolfe declared baby boomers the "Me Generation" on the cover of *New York* magazine, due to our perceived narcissism. In May 2013 Joe Stein accused millennials as "The ME, ME, ME Generation" on the cover of *Time Magazine*, due to their perceived narcissism.

We have symbolized a new interpretation of *E Pluribus Unum*. For some, *"Unum"* meant the individual rather than the group. The division on mask-wearing for protection, receiving or rejecting the vaccines, resulted in some people claiming an assault on their individual rights and freedoms; not what is good for the many, but what is good for *me*.

America is undergoing an equity crisis. This crossroads, one path rationalizing a whitewashed past of the oligarchy from Reagan's Movement Conservatives to Trump's autocracy versus the other path of protesting and voting for change, with Biden's determination to preserve the soul of American democracy for our future, is creating chaos in a country of historical denial.

It may be the embodiment of Representative John Lewis' admonition, "Do not get lost in a sea of despair. Be hopeful, be optimistic. Our struggle is not the struggle of a day, a week, a month, or a year, it is the struggle of a lifetime. Never, ever be afraid to make some noise and get in good trouble, necessary trouble. We will find a way to make a way out of no way."[4]

Intended for taxation and representation purposes only, the three-fifths valuation of enslaved Blacks (Article I, Section 2 of the Constitution) instead inculcated into the psyches of white people proof of white superiority and Black inferiority. Transferred from generation to generation, the exponential damage of this racism is irreparable. America was founded and led by white supremacists; our lands were cleared through genocide; our nation was constructed on the backs of enslaved Blacks and immigrants. Because enslaved Blacks and Indigenous peoples were omitted from the protections of our Constitution, individual rights violations and inequities have continued such that, hundreds of years later, we are once again at the edge of the same abyss that preceded the Civil War.

★ ★ ★ ★ ★

Writing this book was not my idea. My friend Travis Li, a first-generation Chinese American who came to the United States when he was a teenager and too young to have lived through the Civil Rights Protests of the '50s and '60s, became interested in the Black Lives Matter movement and a new term for him, "systemic racism." He could not find answers to his questions. He viewed one of my video presentations on Diversity and Systemic Change and said it helped him better understand what is happening now in America. He convinced me to put my thoughts to paper.

Due to the unexpected necessity of Covid-19 quarantining in 2020, I had time to do the research and the writing. Exploring the major tenets for this book resulted in uncomfortable awakenings to issues I had not anticipated: the sheer brutality and dehumanizing force that was chattel slavery in

America, and its continual punishment of African Americans through systemic racism and other inequities such as the latent superiority ingrained in white individuals growing up in America. I have only scratched the surface of the residual impact of slavery, affecting everyone and everything in our country, and reflected in all our institutions and systems.

We need to inform and educate our youth with the *complete* truth of our United States history, to better prepare the future leaders of this country to address bias and inequities for historically excluded groups. Hopefully, we can put an end to the need for individuals to admit "white privilege" and instead recognize and accept its historical foundation, and how the perpetuation of white superiority has consequences for all of us. We must replace the guilt factor with the responsibilities of American citizenship.

Being an American citizen and swearing allegiance to the Constitution of the United States must include an understanding and acceptance that one inherits America's atrocities as well as the onus to correct them. With the acceptance of rights, we must also accept the responsibilities of citizenship.

Designs of Omission : America's Original Sin* is an introduction to the systematic omissions, missing information, erasures, and "teaching moment" events in our uniquely American history. I hope these examples and tools will enable readers to recognize individual and systemic racism, exclusion and inclusion, so we may work together toward solutions for "a more perfect union" of equality, liberty, and justice for all.

---

* Unless otherwise attributed, quoted and cited, all assessments and conclusions reflect my education and professional career as an international consultant and lecturer in the areas of Organizational Development, Workforce Diversity, Multiculturalism, and Systemic Change. Terminology in the context of *Designs of Omission* theory, concepts, and methodology are capitalized and appear lower case for general usage.

PART ONE

The Constitution of the United States, America's Original Sin

The Constitution of the United States, America's Original Sin

The United States of America is unique. We are a democratic republic with one of the most ethnically and culturally diverse populations on the planet. Our history of revolution, slavery, and early rise to a global leader embodies the perils of hatred, racism, and sexism on the one hand and a reciprocal spirit for indescribable compassion, generosity, courage, and creativity on the other. With our rich and expansive history of success, it is almost unpatriotic to criticize America's evolution into the preeminent democracy in the world. However, if we take a moment to examine our original ethnocentric foundation and our eventual transformation into a multicultural nation, we begin to see the metaphorical cracks in the Liberty Bell.[1]

Most Americans, myself included, are not history buffs and have only a passing comprehension of the details that distinguish the Declaration of Independence from the United States Constitution. The Declaration of Independence was written to inform other nations in the world of our separation from British rule and dominion, enabling individual states to negotiate their trade agreements with other countries. Written eleven years after the Declaration of Independence, the Constitution was a charter establishing three branches of government: executive, legislative, and judicial. It specified the powers, responsibilities, and scope of the federal government, and those of individual states. It was a series of laws, in effect, the supreme law of the land. Tragically, it was a monumental Design of Omission for many of its citizenry.

After winning the battle for its freedom from the British in 1776, America's Second Continental Congress undertook the creation of the Declaration of Independence. Thomas Jefferson wrote the document, which was given to Benjamin Franklin to edit. One change Franklin suggested stands out far more than others. "We hold these truths to be sacred and un-deniable" was changed to "We hold these truths to be self-evident." This distinction is important because the former wording speaks to Jefferson's references to the religious ideologies of the time. In contrast, Franklin's declaration reflects the trending toward indisputable facts of quantification, science, and the law. On July 4, 1776, the Founders declared:

> We hold these truths to be self-evident, that all
> Men are created equal, that they are endowed by
> their Creator with certain unalienable Rights,
> that among these are Life, Liberty and the
> Pursuit of Happiness — That these United
> Colonies are, and of Right ought to be Free
> and Independent States; that they are absolved
> from all Allegiance to the British Crown . . .
> that as Free and Independent States, they have
> full Power to levy War, conclude Peace, contract
> Alliances, and to do all other Acts and Things
> which Independent States may of right do.[2]

Thomas Jefferson has been criticized as a hypocrite for writing "all Men are created equal,"[3] while owning over 600 individuals and producing six children with his enslaved mistress, Sally Hemings.[4] The phrase reflects the status of mankind before his God, religious freedom, rather than the social construct of citizenship. Jefferson was a visionary, writing not only for himself or then-current times, but instead expressing his hope for the future. While assuming that slavery would not continue forever, he was envisioning a day *not* when Black men would be considered equal to white men, but when non-landed gentry white men would be considered equal by birth to landed gentry white men.

The founding of the United States of America, separating itself from Britain with the Declaration of Independence and unifying its thirteen colonies, was a hopeful and idealistic belief in a new and equitable society. However, the scripting of the Constitution of the United States sanctioned the Original Sin which I believe was not malicious in intent, but instead the result of an ignorant assumption that white Anglo-Saxon Christian Founders could be the architects of a diverse society in an unimagined future.

The Founders unintentionally committed the Original Sin of creating documents, laws, requirements, and citizenship, using themselves as the sole criteria for participation. They assumed that people who followed in their footsteps would be similar to themselves and created systems and institutions based upon that fallacy. Systemic exclusion is the predictable consequence of the creative process of self-inclusion.

In my professional experience, the designers of all programs, institutions and systems follow the logical process of mirroring themselves, or people like themselves, to determine the criteria for participation. Exclusions are already embedded in the design by the time the procedures of participation and execution are created, ultimately reflecting the designers' preferences and biases, absent the creation of options or allowances for the participation of individuals different from the designers. The Framers' concerns were primarily that the policies be equitable, just, universally accepted, and legal.

Despite the recurring social uprisings revealing our fundamental human flaws of greed, corruption, and xenophobia, America simultaneously possesses the perpetual remedy to these imperfections. That is the Constitution of the United States written in 1787, ratified in 1788, and functioning since 1789. It is the world's longest surviving written charter of government. Its initial three words, "We the People," affirm that the government exists to serve its citizens. It has been amended 27 times, most recently in 1992. The first ten amendments constitute the Bill of Rights of all American citizens. These rights were not accorded to enslaved Blacks, Indigenous peoples, or to women.[5]

> We the People of the United States, in Order
> to form a more perfect Union, establish Justice,
> insure domestic Tranquility, provide for the
> common defense, promote the general Welfare,
> and secure the Blessings of Liberty to ourselves
> and our Posterity, do ordain and establish this
> Constitution for the United States of America.[6]

The Framers of the Constitution established justice based not upon a set of principles, but upon a set of laws, to address the balance of power within the federal government and the extent of its control over state governments. It primarily protected individuals and property, therein legalizing human enslavement and slave trading, a fundamental component of the economy of southern states. In addressing the issue of the number of members in the House of Representatives per state, Article I, Section 2, declares:

Representatives and direct Taxes shall be
apportioned among the several States which
may be included within this Union, according
to their respective Numbers, which shall be
determined by adding to the whole Number of
free Persons, including those bound to Service
for a Term of Years, and *excluding Indians not
taxed, three fifths of all other Persons.*[7]

This Design of Omission, The Constitution of the United States, omitted enslaved Blacks, Native Americans, and women from citizenship. It excluded all individuals unlike the Founders in physical appearance, language, cultural background, religion, and philosophy, resulting in the phenomenon that, as an excluded group, one did not legally or systemically exist.

When an individual is recognized as an entity, the Constitution obligates the previously-excluded to modify themselves to appear similar to the preexisting criteria for participation. Excluded groups must first be accepted, then accommodated, in order to participate. The system itself does not change to include them; instead, it requires that excluded groups must change themselves in an attempt to retrofit into a system that was not designed to include them.

Exclusion is the epitome of discrimination because it means that systemically one does not exist, which results in the following conundrum: the Constitution protects the rights of individuals, but exclusion is a group factor. As a member of an excluded group, an individual is seen and judged as the group, without the benefit of one's individual rights.

It also means that the creation of Civil Rights legislation for the protection of excluded groups is fundamentally unconstitutional because it responds to the need for group rights. Racism is a group bias establishing a barrier against what should be a very simple resolution of constitutional conflict among individual rights. However, it is virtually impossible to solve a problem when the factor causing the problem does not exist in the original design. In this case, the group is the factor, but the solution is expressed in the same terms as those for individual rights.

The assumption that an individual or group is capable of designing a Constitution, government, institution or system that will be fair and equitable for all individuals, including those from different ethnic or cultural groups or "others" never anticipated at the time, was naive. Designs of Omission inevitably result in the product or outcome of exclusion. Failing to recognize that diverse individuals, representative of all, must participate in the design to achieve equity and inclusion has been costly. Unfortunately, the Constitution is the foundation of policies that determine merit, qualification, and eligibility, resulting in exclusion in all our institutions and systems.

The fact that the Constitution is an amendable document, adaptable to unanticipated changes in America's citizenry, is its greatest attribute. Being modifiable is important because it is a reminder that we can always do better. As a living document, it must at times be amended to reflect its people and transformed circumstances. It has not been an easy, popular, or painless evolution to the 21st Century. Aiming for a true reflection of "We the People" necessitated the following strides toward equity and equality resulting from omissions in the original design of the Constitution of the United States:

1865 ⋆ **13th Amendment** to the Constitution granted freedom to enslaved people.

1868 ⋆ **14th Amendment** granted the enslaved "full citizenship," without the right to vote.

1870 ⋆ **15th Amendment** granted Black men the right to vote.

1920 ⋆ **19th Amendment** granted white women the right to vote.

1924 ⋆ **Indian Citizenship Act** granted Native Americans the right to vote.

1943 ⋆ **Magnuson Act** granted Chinese Americans the right to vote.

1964 ⋆ **Civil Rights Act** ended segregation in public places and banned employment discrimination based on race, color, religion, sex, or national origin; it did not include voting rights of Black and Latinx women, nor protect people with disabilities. Discrimination against people with disabilities would not be addressed until 1973, when Section 504 of the Rehabilitation Act of 1973 became law, and later still in 1990, when the ADA was passed.

1965 ⋆ **Voting Rights Act** granted Black and Latinx women the right to vote.

1975 ⋆ **Voting Rights Act** was amended to include "language minority citizens."

1984 ⋆ **Voting Accessibility for Elderly and Handicapped Act Law** was passed.

Since specific differences among excluded participants are rarely considered or addressed in creating a system, the omissions in our Constitution resulted in the need for modifications and accommodations. However, without systemic change via amendments through legislation or executive order, lateral attempts at inclusion such as Separate But Equal or Affirmative Action have not provided fundamental equality.

Another dilemma of exclusion is that the system must decide whether to accept or reject an individual previously not been considered a legal participant. White Europeans were the norm in America, so what to do about enslaved Blacks when they were emancipated? Next came the problem of integrating non-European immigrants into the mainstream of America.

A fully equitable society begins with the expansion of the criteria for legal inclusion. A society for all is one in which every individual, each with rights and responsibilities, has an active role to play. America's Original Sin was the legal omission and thereby exclusion of Blacks, Native Americans, and women from our Constitution, preventing their full participation in our systems and institutions, resulting in inequity and discrimination.

The problem is exclusion; the solution is inclusion, by expanding the criteria for participation. Since this issue has yet to be addressed systemically, it continues to plague us today. Exclusion is a *product* of a Design of Omission. It cannot be eliminated by mere representation of diversity. Inclusion is a *process* promoting change and constant improvement, implemented by a design model that allows total participation of individuals and groups by expanding the model's criteria for participation.

The metaphor of being unable to place a square
peg into a round hole illustrates the problem.
The Separate but Equal solution would be to
create a square hole for the square peg; the
inclusion solution is to expand the criteria for
participation by expanding the hole so any shape
will pass through, making the hole large enough
so that round, square, rectangle, and triangles
— *all shapes* — will fit.

While I do not believe that these omissions were en-
acted with malice, the intent, although absent, was evident.
There is no mention of slavery or African Americans in the
Constitution. This omission was not a consensus on the mo-
rality of slavery. Instead, it reflected the economic and political conflicts of the slavery industry as evidenced in the
contentious debates among the Framers of the Constitution
and early citizens of the Union, which ultimately resulted in
the American Civil War.

PART TWO

Introduction to
A History of Systemic Exclusion

Introduction to
A History of Systemic Exclusion

*W*e are embarking on a quest for truth and racial justice. "'In the beginning,' Englishman John Locke wrote, 'all the world was America.' In America, everything became a beginning."[1] Recognizing the omissions of slavery, Indigenous peoples, and non-European immigration is crucial to understanding the history, construction, and economic development of our nation.

North America was populated by Indigenous peoples prior to the formation of the United States of America. Between 1500 and 1800, approximately two and a half million Europeans immigrated to the Americas, resulting in a genocide of fifty million Native Americans, chiefly from foreign diseases such as smallpox, to which the Natives had no immunity. Next, twelve million Africans were kidnapped and delivered by force, sold into the industry of slavery as free labor.[2]

With the exception of Indigenous Americans, Alaska Natives, Native Hawaiians, and Pacific Islanders, America is a nation of immigrants. The statement is often used to counter white supremacists when they mythologize a country exclusively or predominantly white, an erasure of the true story of America.

The idealized American immigrant story invokes the elusive "American Dream" while ignoring the existence of First Nations and enslaved Blacks who were already present, in denial of experiences such as the Cherokee Trail of

Tears demonstrating their history of coercion and genocide, or that of the Great Migration of African Americans north and westward to escape the terror of the Jim Crow South.

Compared with some of our international counterparts, a critical difference in America is the absence of responsibility for the genocide of Indigenous Native Americans; the torture, rape, and murder of Blacks since slavery; and the hatred and internment of our Japanese citizens. These crimes fall upon the shoulders of our leadership, as well as upon the American citizenry. Our legacy of bigotry and racism continues to thrive today. "We the People" currently translates to "We, *some of* the People."

* * * * *

CHAPTER 1

Indigenous Peoples, Native Americans

*I*mmigration to this country first occurred thousands of years before Europeans began crossing the Atlantic by ship and settling *en masse*. America's earliest immigrants were Native American ancestors who crossed a narrow piece of land connecting Asia to North America some 20,000 years ago during the last Ice Age.

From 1609 to 1924, Native Americans fought wars to keep the lands they occupied before the arrival of European *emigres* and America's Founders. Theirs has been a story of suffering, deprivation, wars, and genocide. Legal battles over their native lands and rights continue to this day.

The forced relocation of thousands of Native Americans from their homelands to areas west of the Mississippi River in 1838 is one of the darkest events in American history. The "Trail of Tears" march resulted in the deaths of thousands of Native Americans from numerous tribes, including the Cherokee, Seminole, Choctaw, and Chickasaw, primarily due to disease and exposure to frigid weather. In 1890, the Battle of Wounded Knee, South Dakota, was the last major conflict between Native American and U.S. soldiers slaughtering approximately three hundred Sioux.

Congress established the Department of the Interior in 1849 to oversee domestic policy of the United States including control of Indian affairs and public lands. As white settlers encroached upon Indigenous territory, the government seized their lands through treaties, promising the tribes food, clothing, shelter, education, health care, tools, and seeds to become farmers, plus annual cash subsidies. These goods and money were purported to replace the livelihoods the tribes lost, *not payments to purchase their lands.* Tribes were herded onto reservations and overseen by an agent.

By the twentieth century, the Department of the Interior was managing mineral and grazing rights on Indigenous land and federally-owned land. Federal law permitted companies to claim the minerals under land they staked out. After discovering oil in the West, President Taft issued an executive order protecting more than three million acres of public lands in California and Wyoming, reserving the oil under them for use by the U.S. Navy. Congress passed the Mineral Leasing Act in 1920, charging the Interior Department with overseeing leases to explore for oil and minerals, permit drilling and mining, and receive payments for anything extracted.

Indigenous peoples did not become citizens until The Citizenship Act of 1934, granting American citizenship to "all non-citizen Indians born within the territorial limits of the United States." What could be more natural than natives inhabiting lands renamed the United States of America *not* being required to go through a naturalization process?

The American Indian Movement (AIM) was founded in 1968 by Native American leaders as a militant political and civil rights organization. They planned the occupation of Wounded Knee, site of the infamous massacre of 300 Sioux by the 7th Cavalry in 1890, as a means of forcing the federal government to investigate the corruption on the Pine Ridge Reservation and other reservations, the Bureau of Indian Affairs, and the broken Indian treaties with the U.S. government. AIM members occupied Alcatraz Island off San Francisco from November 1969-1971, claiming rights under a treaty provision granting them unused federal land.

On February 27, 1973, some 200 AIM-led Sioux seized control of Wounded Knee, taking eleven hostages, as local authorities and federal agents descended upon the Pine Ridge Reservation. The AIM members traded gunfire with the Federal Marshals surrounding the settlement. After 71 days of fighting with the Federal Government and the loss of many lives, including two FBI employees, armed members of AIM surrendered to the federal authorities. Violence continued.

The United States' longest serving political prisoner, Native American activist Leonard Peltier, has been behind bars for the past 45 years for a crime he says he didn't commit. He was accused of killing two FBI agents during another shootout on Pine Ridge Reservation in South Dakota in 1975, sentenced to two consecutive life sentences, and denied parole. His imprisonment has been denounced by Pope Francis, Nelson Mandela, the Dalai Lama, and others. Many expected former President Bill Clinton to grant him clemency, but neither he nor subsequent presidents have done so.

Peltier is gravely ill with diseases not treatable within our prison system and has contracted Covid. Former prosecutor James Reynolds sent a letter to President Joe Biden asking him to commute Peltier's sentence, saying that the government did not have evidence "to prove that Mr Peltier personally committed any offence. . . . I write today from a position rare for a former prosecutor: to beseech you to commute the sentence of a man who I helped put behind bars."[3]

Kent Blansett, Langston Hughes Associate Professor of Indigenous Studies and History at the University of Kansas, Cherokee, Creek, Choctaw, Shawnee, and Potawatomi descendant and author of *A Journey to Freedom: Richard Oakes, Alcatraz, and the Red Power Movement*, claims that now is the time to reexamine this travesty of human rights, the failed

race relations that have forged themselves into our government systems, and to award clemency to the targeted and
wrongly imprisoned Leonard Peltier.[4]

* * * * *

During the 1970-1980 period, I was contracted to
work with the Lakota (Sioux) Indian tribe on Pine Ridge,
South Dakota. This was my introduction to Indian Reservation Tribes, and I was unprepared for the conditions and restrictions for my safety. I was housed in a trailer with Indian
guards and not allowed to go anywhere unaccompanied by
the Lakota people.

I was there to help the Lakota tribe negotiate terms
with the school board for the schools on the reservation.
Even though the schools were on the reservation, they were
managed by non-Indian school board members, an example
of the U.S. government intervening and establishing control
of Indian school systems.

The problem was the illiteracy and dropout rates of
the Indian children. The school board claimed the failures
were cultural, an Indian issue. The reservation schools had a
dropout rate over 70% after the 10th grade.

I helped the tribe to build the case that some cultural
influences could cause a failure in education of 30-40%, but
a 70% failure was a systemic failure. I evaluated the materials for cultural content, teaching methodologies for cultural
practices, and community involvement procedures. I advised
them to present the case as one of the absences of culturally
relevant information, participation, and methodology due to
the systemic failure of the school system.

The Lakotas won their lawsuit because the school board
was unprepared to address their itemized concerns, caught

off guard by the specific assessments and recommendations presented. The ruling resulted in requiring that the majority on the school board must be residents of the Pine Ridge Reservation. It also required culturally sensitive inclusion of the school curriculum and methodologies. And, yes, the tribe got me out of town before the final decision came in.

I visited my co-member of the Multicultural Drug Prevention Advisory Board, Wanda Frogg. Her husband was a chief on the Chippewa reservation in Wisconsin. I had the opportunity to participate in a Sweat Lodge Ceremony where I experienced claustrophobia, survived and learned a great deal. I had a taste of grits and grease, which, unfortunately, I really enjoyed. I learned that the Indians on the Reservation called the local Walmart, fifty miles away, "Indian Heaven" because it had everything they could ever want or need.

I also conducted a consultation and training on the Window Rock Navajo Reservation. It was another awakening to different cultural norms. Our meeting was scheduled to begin at 9 a.m. on the given day. By 10:30 a.m. there were only three people present. I asked where the rest of the members were. The response was, "They will be here . . . *today.*" I did not realize how large the reservation was and that some participants had to drive hundreds of miles. They literally meant we would start "today."

I remember a very significant interaction when the lead Navajo representative asked me why the white men who were trying to purchase some of the Navajo lands to mine for minerals and natural resources such as oil could not comprehend their answer, *"We cannot sell our mother earth because no one truly owns it."* The aspiring buyers kept asking and trying to negotiate a price. I suggested they ask the buyers what would be the price for them to sell their mothers to the

Navajo. I then told the Navajos not to be surprised if they got a price. The Navajos later informed me they had shared that story many times and still got a great laugh out of it.

* * * * *

An example of the process of inclusion was the 2021 Biden administration appointment of Representative Deb Haaland (D-NM) as Native American Secretary of the Interior (including the nation's 574 federally-recognized American Indian, Alaskan Native communities, and the Bureau of Indian Affairs). Member of the Laguna Pueblo Nation, whose people had lived on the land that is now New Mexico for 35 generations, daughter of two military veterans, Haaland had earned a law degree and was a tribal leader focused on environmentally responsible economic development for the Lagunas before she became a Democratic leader.[5]

During confirmation hearings, a Republican Senator from Wyoming on the Senate Energy and Natural Resources Committee declared that his state collected more than a billion dollars a year in royalties and taxes from the oil, gas, and coal produced on federal lands. Haaland responded that having "lived most of my adult life paycheck to paycheck," she understood the economic struggles of ordinary Americans, and vowed "to responsibly manage our natural resources to protect them for future generations, so that we can continue to work, live, hunt, fish, and pray among them. A voice like mine has never been a Cabinet secretary or at the head of the Department of Interior. I'll be fierce for all of us, our planet, and all of our protected land."[6]

CHAPTER 2

African American Racism in America

"*B*enjamin Franklin, like many an American after him, lost his trademark equanimity when it came to the question of color." Reckoning with that racial line, he added one more observation to his essay on population, writing about a new race, a people who were "white."

"The Number of purely white People in the World is proportionably very small," Franklin began. As he saw it, Africans were "[B]lack;" Asians and Native Americans were "tawny;" Spaniards, Italians, French, Russians, Swedes, and Germans were "swarthy."That left very few people, and chiefly the English, as the only "white people" in the world. "I could wish their Numbers were increased," Franklin said, adding, wonderingly, "But perhaps I am partial to the Complexion of my Country, for such Kind of Partiality is natural to Mankind." [1]

Slavery, the Foundation of Racism,
or Racism, the Foundation of Slavery?

America's booming economy and resultant world leadership were built upon the backs of the enslaved, free labor to further enrich a wealthy elite in the agrarian plantation South. Kidnapped off the coast of West Africa as early as August 1619, these involuntary immigrants became the foundation of an irresolvable national institution and ideology, that of systemic racism in America. "America begins in [B]lack plunder and white democracy, two features that are not contradictory but complementary. 'The men who came together to found the independent United States, dedicated to freedom and equality, either held slaves or were willing to join hands with those who did,' wrote historian Edmund S. Morgan.[2]

While slavery was a fundamentally divisive issue for the Framers of the Constitution, they miraculously ensured a future of systemic racism without ever using the term in the document. In his *Two Treatises on Government*, John Locke wrote: "Slavery is so vile and miserable an estate of man, and so directly opposite to the generous temper and courage of our nation, that it is hardly to be conceived that an Englishman, much less a gentleman, should plead for it." He argued that all men are born equal, and that slavery was no part either of a state of nature or of civil society. Yet his Carolinas constitution read "Every Freeman of Carolina shall have absolute power and Authority over his Negro slaves."[3]

"Property requirements meant that not all free white men could vote . . . that slaves could be manumitted by their masters meant that it was possible to be both [B]lack and free and white and unfree. By 1680, 'these two words, Negro and Slave' had grown Homogeneous and [fungible]: to be [B]lack was to be a slave."[4] The only justification for the contradiction of some people being born free while others were not was the introduction of a new concept, an ideology of race. Race is a fiction, a social construct. Racism is an attitude or belief that Anglos are superior to people of color. America has been a racist republic from its inception.

Slavery was the critical divide in the framing of the Constitution. The entangled calculations of the enslaved as property reflecting wealth and the population they represented as individuals resulted in the ten-year federal census. Slavery almost prevented the union of the thirteen colonies and resulted in the Civil War. The foundation of systemic racism is the institution of slavery and the Constitution's promotion of unequal value of human life of Africans compared with whites. The crucial point is that slavery affected the social evolution of both Blacks and whites in the formation and development of America.

While the three-fifths valuation of Blacks was a formula for determining the number of representatives each state could elect to the federal House of Representatives, it resulted in unexpected non-racial ramifications when northern populations grew faster than the South, giving the North greater representation in Congress.

The North, via taxation of the wealthy, wanted to develop infrastructure, invest in education, and create a department of agriculture. The South did not need infrastructure development and recognized that their political capital in the federal government was dwindling. They wanted to shrink the size and scope of the federal government and expand states' rights. The Missouri Compromise in 1820 and The Indian Removal Act of 1830 created a competition that could only result in a civil war.[5]

The lack of access to factual information about the history and institution of slavery, its social and economic impacts in the South and, after The Great Migration, in the North and West of the United States, is a barrier to resolving systemic racism.

The New York Times Magazine created "The 1619 Project" in 2019 to coincide with the 400th anniversary of the 1619 arrival of enslaved Africans in Virginia colony, an interactive commemoration which "aims to reframe the country's history by placing the consequences of slavery and the contributions of Black Americans at the very center of [the United States'] national narrative." It was directed by journalist Nikole Hannah-Jones, who received the 2020 Pulitzer Prize for Commentary for her introductory essay on Democracy. "White Americans desire to be free of a past they do not want to remember, while Black Americans remain bound to a past they can never forget." (As a consequence, the conservative white management at the University of North Carolina denied her tenure, exemplifying a thriving institutional racism.)[6] Historians, social scientists, and literary authors have produced a large body of work and testament that racism can be traced directly to America's history of slavery.

A Civil War, Emancipation, and Hatred

We were taught that the Civil War was fought over the moral issue of slavery; however, it was the economics and political control of that southern industry that were the heart of the conflict and resulted in the bloodiest war in the history of North America.

The Declaration of Independence made no mention of rights, instead speaking to principles, religion, and hierarchy. The Constitution declared individual rights, a body of laws, and established justice. It protected not human rights, instead those of property, effectively a legalization of human enslavement.

By 1820 northern states had emancipated their enslaved, although still profiting from slavery in the South. The South needed free labor to perform the work of the cotton and tobacco plantations. With the establishment of quantification of slave representation in the House, the South was losing government control to the North's rapidly growing population. Two Senators represented each state, but the number of Representatives was calculated on population.

The southern elite considered taxation a redistribution of wealth from prosperous white landowners to poor whites, Blacks, and other people of color, a form of socialism. They maintained that allowing money to move upwards was a social benefit, that the wealthy would use their assets as stewards of society.

A dominant issue between the North and South was states' rights. The southern states wanted to assert their authority over the federal government so they could abolish federal laws they didn't support, especially laws interfering with the South's right to own slaves and take them wherever they wished. Another critical factor was territorial expansion. The South wanted to take slavery into the western territories, while the North was committed to keeping expansion open to white labor alone.[7]

Meanwhile, the newly formed Republican party, whose members strongly opposed the westward expansion of slavery into new states, was gaining prominence. The election of Republican Abraham Lincoln as President in 1860 sealed the deal. Without a single southern electoral vote, his victory was a clear signal to the southern states that they had lost all influence.

Feeling excluded from the political system, they turned to the only alternative they believed was left to them: secession, a political decision that led directly to war. The Confederate States of America was formed, with Jefferson Davis sworn in as President in February 1861. Abraham Lincoln was inaugurated as President of the United States March 4, 1861.[8]

Lincoln issued a preliminary decree in September 1862 stating that unless rebellious states returned to the Union by January 1, freedom would be granted to the enslaved within those states. The decree also offered compensated emancipation. No Confederate states took the offer. It is important to note that while President Lincoln detested the idea of slavery, he did not contemplate a racially integrated American society. He imagined that Blacks would form their own colony or leave America to resettle elsewhere.[9]

President Lincoln issued the Emancipation Proclamation on January 1, 1863 as the nation approached its third year of war. The proclamation declared "that all persons held as slaves" within the rebellious states "are, and henceforward shall be free."

The Emancipation Proclamation did not free all enslaved individuals in the United States, declaring free only those living in states *not* under Union control. "We show our sympathy with slavery by emancipating slaves where we cannot reach them and holding them in bondage where we can set them free."[10] Lincoln was fully aware of the irony, but he did not want to antagonize the slave states loyal to the Union by setting their enslaved free. The proclamation also allowed Black soldiers to fight for the Union, who desperately needed additional soldiers, thereby associating the issue of slavery directly to the Civil War.

While the Emancipation Proclamation legally freed Blacks, it simultaneously heightened racist beliefs among white slaveholders and those whites not wealthy enough to own enslaved Blacks. Laws do not change attitudes, beliefs, and feelings of superiority. Feelings of superiority are the foundation of systemic racism and the genesis of latent racist beliefs in whites throughout America.

After four brutal years of conflict, the United States defeated the Confederate States; 618,222 men died in the Civil War, 360,222 from the North, and 258,000 from the

South. In the end, the states in rebellion were readmitted to the United States, and the institution of slavery was abolished nationwide.

On April 9, 1865 southern General Robert E. Lee surrendered at Appomattox Court House, Virginia. On April 14, 1865, President Abraham Lincoln was assassinated in Washington, D.C. "This country was formed for the white, not for the [B]lack man," wrote John Wilkes Booth, before killing Abraham Lincoln. "And looking upon African slavery from the same standpoint held by those noble Framers of our Constitution, I for one have ever considered it one of the greatest blessings (both for themselves and us) that God ever bestowed upon a favored nation." [11]

The period after the Civil War was a wave of terrorism in the South. "For the next century, political violence was visited upon [B]lacks wantonly, with special treatment meted out toward [B]lack people of ambition. Black schools and churches were burned to the ground. Black voters and the political candidates who attempted to rally them were intimidated, and some were murdered." [12]

The wealth accorded America by slavery was not just in what the enslaved pulled from the land but in the population itself. "In 1860, slaves as an asset were worth more than all of America's manufacturing, all of the railroads, all of the productive capacity of the United States put together," noted Yale historian David W. Blight. "Slaves were the single largest, by far, financial asset of property in the entire American economy." The sale of these slaves ". . . in whose bodies that money congealed," wrote Harvard historian Walter Johnson, generated even more ancillary wealth. Loans were taken out for purchase, to be repaid with interest. Insurance policies were drafted against the untimely death of a slave and the loss of potential profits. Slave sales were taxed and notarized. The vending of the [B]lack body and the sundering of the [B]lack family became an economy unto themselves, estimated to have brought tens of millions of dollars to antebellum America. In 1860 there were more millionaires per capita in the Mississippi Valley than anywhere else in the country.[13]

Wall Street and slavery were interconnected. The street was named for the wall built along the river to protect New York City from invasion. Slave labor built the wall and much of the city. Slave auctions were held at the foot of Wall Street when ships carrying enslaved Africans arrived. Several contemporary institutions, Lehman Brothers, Wachovia Bank, Chase Manhattan, and Aetna Inc., share a history of financial success based on the slave trade.

In 1781, Wachovia Bank of North Carolina was founded on the profits of the slave trade. It made loans to slave owners and accepted the enslaved as collateral. When owners defaulted on the loans, the bank became the new slave owner.

The Lehman family members were Alabaman cotton brokers and owned slaves to build their wealth before moving to New York and establishing the New York Cotton Exchange in 1870.

The Morgan family of Massachusetts became a major stock broker. Chase bank was owned by the Rockefeller family. Eventually, they merged to become JP Morgan-Chase. They also made loans to slave owners and accepted 13,000 enslaved Africans as collateral. The banks acquired their fortunes by becoming the new owners of 1,250 slaves when owners defaulted.

Another profitable company was Aetna Insurance Company which sold insurance to owners to protect their investments in human cargo aboard the slave ships and on the plantation, should a slave die. These life insurance policies issued in the 1850s compensated slave owners for the loss of humans considered property (chattels) at that time.

Slavery assured that these capitalistic enterprises became profitable and powerful. The foundation of American capitalism was created by the industry of slave labor and racism. The racism that developed from the perspective of the economic benefit of slavery thus became institutional. After the Civil War, the United States progressed from competitive capitalism to imperialism and became a financial empire.[14]

The resolution of the Civil War created the need for the 13th, 14th, and 15th Amendments to the Constitution, to address the newly-formulated status of freed slaves and to assist the South to rebuild during Reconstruction due to their loss of free slave labor. It is important to note that the refusal to comply with these amendments resulted in the Jim Crow Laws of the South and the racial injustice that still haunts us today.

Post-Emancipation Jim Crow South

The segregation and disenfranchisement laws known as "Jim Crow" were a formal codified system of racial apartheid to remove political and economic gains made by Black people during the Reconstruction period. These state and local Jim Crow Laws, the legislation of institutional racism, mandated racial segregation of public schools, parks, libraries, drinking fountains, restrooms, buses, trains, and restaurants. "Whites Only" and "Colored" signs were constant reminders of the enforced racial order between white and Black people and were enforced until 1965.[15]

After 250 years of enslavement, emancipation did not free Black people. "They were terrorized. In the Deep South, a second slavery ruled. In the North, legislatures, mayors, civic associations, banks, and citizens all colluded to pin Black people into ghettos, where they were overcrowded, overcharged, and undereducated. Businesses discriminated against them, awarding them the worst jobs and the worst wages. Police brutalized them in the streets. And the notion that [B]lack lives, [B]lack bodies, and [B]lack wealth were rightful targets remained deeply rooted in the broader society.... For the next 250 years, American law worked to reduce [B]lack people to a class of untouchables and raise all white men to the level of citizens. . . . Nearly 4,000 African-Americans were lynched by white mobs in the Jim Crow South from 1877 to 1950."[16]

In theory, Blacks received Separate but Equal treatment under the law. In actuality, public facilities for Blacks were nearly always inferior to those for whites, when they existed at all. Also, Blacks, some with college degrees, were systematically denied the right to vote in most of the rural South. These voting barriers were selective racially motivated impromptu requirements such as literacy tests, or reciting specific Amendments to the Constitution, even randomly conceived tests like guessing the number of gumballs in a jar, all of which they were preordained to fail, as they were monitored by white registrars.

Institutional Racism Becomes Systemic

Economist and attorney Heather McGhee stated in her book *The Sum of Us: What Racism Costs Everyone and How We can Prosper Together* that the zero-sum mindset that progress for people of color comes at the expense of white people is a lie. Aggressively sold to white Americans by people vested in the economic status quo and in keeping the concentration of wealth and power very narrowly held, she argued that racism is harmful to everyone. When laws and practices discriminated against Blacks, whites were also harmed. Data show that white Americans, more than Americans of color, are threatened by the idea of demographic change and shun policies in their economic interest. For example, the majority of those making under $15 an hour are white. The majority of people without health care are white.[17]

She explained how the U.S. government took steps in the mid-20th century to create a middle class, albeit a predominantly white middle class. The discrimination against Blacks in the implementation of the GI bill for college education and the Veterans Administration home loan benefits effectively blocked the creation of intergenerational wealth intended by public policy from the New Deal through the Civil Rights movement. Few note that Roosevelt's New Deal rested on the foundation of Jim Crow. This cumulative intergenerational disadvantage resulted in the phenomenal racial wealth gap we have today. "Old-age insurance (Social Security proper) and unemployment insurance excluded farmworkers and domestics—jobs heavily occupied by [B]lacks. When President Roosevelt signed Social Security into law in 1935, 65 percent of African Americans nationally and between 70 and 80 percent in the South were ineligible. The [National Association for the Advancement of Colored People] NAACP protested, calling the new American safety net 'a sieve with holes just big enough for the majority of Negroes to fall through.'"[18]

A parable of the book is what McGhee called the Americanization project whereby the United States went on a building boom from the 1920s to the '40s creating bath-temperature "melting pots" of grand resort-style swimming pools. When desegregation efforts were made in the 1950s and '60s, white towns facing integration orders from courts preferred to drain their public swimming pools rather than let Black families swim, too. In 1958, Montgomery, Alabama, backed in a truck to fill the pool with dirt and paved it over. They also sold the animals in the municipal zoo, closing Montgomery's entire parks and recreation department for a decade.[19]

One of the most blatant examples of racism ultimately costing everyone was the recount of the financial crash of 2008. The wealth of median Black families shrank by more than half between 2005 and 2009. At the end of an NPR interview, McGhee commented that she was in law school in 2008 when she saw that Lehman Brothers was going into bankruptcy, having invested the most in mortgage-backed securities right at the end of the bubble. "And it wasn't until I was writing this book that I learned that Lehman Brothers, the original brothers Lehman, were slaveholders who made their money in the Confederacy, running cotton behind the cotton blockade during the war and setting up the cotton stock exchange and just how tied up it all is." [20]

In 2001, the *Associated Press* published a three-part investigation into the theft of Black-owned land dating back to the antebellum period. They documented 406 victims and 24,000 acres of land valued at tens of millions of dollars obtained by means ranging from legal chicanery to terrorism.[21]

From the 1930s through the 1960s, Blacks were institutionally and systemically deprived of legitimate home mortgages. They were offered only contract sales made with the seller, not with a bank. These were predatory agreements where the seller kept the deed until the contract was paid in full. Unlike a typical mortgage, owners accrued no equity. If the buyer/owner missed a single payment, they immediately forfeited the down payment, all monthly payments to date, as well as the property itself. Some properties were sold multiple times.

Congress created the Federal Housing Administration (FHA) in 1934. The FHA adopted a mapping system: green = "A" indicating prestigious neighborhoods lacking "a single foreigner or Negro," thus excellent prospects for insurance. Neighborhoods where Blacks lived were marked red = "D" indicating properties ineligible for FHA loans.[22]

"A government offering such bounty to builders and lenders could have required compliance with a nondiscrimination policy," Charles Abrams, the urban-studies expert who helped create the New York City Housing Authority, wrote in 1955. "Instead, the FHA adopted a racial policy that could well have been culled from the Nuremberg laws."[23]

Redlining went beyond FHA-backed loans and spread throughout the entire mortgage industry, already rife with racism. Contract sellers used every tool at their disposal to pilfer from their clients. They scared white residents into selling low. They lied about properties' compliance with building codes, then left the buyer responsible when city inspectors arrived. They presented themselves as real-estate brokers, when in fact, they were the owners. They guided their clients to lawyers who were in on the scheme.

Ta Nehisi Coates noted, "Blacks were herded into the sights of unscrupulous lenders who took them for money and for sport." "It was like people who like to go out and shoot lions in Africa. It was the same thrill," a housing attorney told historian Beryl Satter in her 2009 book, *Family Properties*. "The thrill of the chase and the kill."[24]

Eighty-five percent of Black homeowners bought on contract. FHA appraisers low-balled the value of their properties. White flight continued as contract sellers became rich. Black communities became ghettos. Melvin L. Oliver and Thomas M. Shapiro, in their 1995 book, *Black Wealth/White Wealth*, outlined the devastation. Blacks were locked out of the foremost mass-based opportunity for wealth accumulation in American history, in large part accounting for the dramatic wealth gap today.

The Civil Rights Act of 1964

In April 1963 Dr. Martin Luther King wrote *Letter from Birmingham Jail* in solitary confinement. "Perhaps it is easy for those who have never felt the stinging darts of segregation to say, 'Wait,' but when you have seen vicious mobs lynch your mothers and fathers at will and drown your sisters and brothers at whim; when you have seen hate-filled policemen curse, kick and even kill your Black brothers and sisters; when you see the vast majority of your twenty million Negro brothers smothering in an airtight cage of poverty in the midst of an affluent society . . . then you will understand why we find it difficult to wait." [25]

In July 1963, President Kennedy addressed the nation on television, "If an American, because his skin is dark, cannot eat lunch in a restaurant open to the public; if he cannot send his children to the best public school available; if he cannot vote for the public officials who represent him; if, in short, he cannot enjoy the full and free life which all of us want, then who among us would be content to have the color of his skin change and stand in his place? One hundred years of delay have passed since President Lincoln freed the slaves, yet their heirs, their grandsons, are not fully free." [26]

President Kennedy was assassinated on November 22, 1963 leaving President Lyndon B. Johnson to sign into law the Civil Rights Act 1964, which (1) outlawed discrimination based on race, color, religion, sex, or national origin; (2) gave the Attorney General power to enforce desegregation; (3) allowed for civil rights cases to move from state to federal courts; and (4) expanded the Civil Rights Commission. "No memorial oration or eulogy could more eloquently honor President Kennedy's memory than the earliest possible passage of the civil rights bill for which he fought so long." [27]

The 1965 Immigration and Nationality Act combined with quotas by nation of origin in the National Origins Act of 1924, elevating immigration to front and center, adjacent to the Civil Rights Movement in public and political debate.

However, the Civil Rights Act and the Civil Rights Movement accomplished little towards compensating for the intergenerational wealth gap and the safety of Black citizens today. Police executed two hundred Black citizens between the George Floyd murder in 2020 and the Derek Chauvin trial verdict in 2021.[28] America demonstrates the exclusion that permeates its institutions and systems and illustrates that accommodations to date do not yet afford "liberty and justice for all."

Omissions and Erasures

The Red Summer of 1919. After World War I and the Great Migration, some one million African Americans fled segregation and lack of economic opportunities in the South for the North. Between 1910 and 1920, Chicago's Black population in increased by 148 percent and Philadelphia's by 500 percent, creating massive anxiety among whites in northern cities (who were already weathering an economic recession) that Blacks were taking their jobs, housing, and security.

At the end of World War I, Black veterans returning to their homes were assaulted for daring to wear the American uniform. The demobilization of soldiers after the war, which put white and Black veterans into competition for scarce jobs, resulted in the Red Summer of 1919: a succession of racist pogroms in cities across the nation. Although the riots were sparked by disparate events, the common denominator was racial hatred against people who had recently risen out of enslavement and prospered. Blacks were tortured, dismembered, lynched, and set afire by barbaric white mobs in Omaha, Nebraska; St. Louis, Missouri; Longview, Texas; Washington, D.C.; Chicago, Illinois; Elaine, Arkansas; and Tulsa, Oklahoma.[29]

"Because of their military service, [B]lack veterans were seen as a particular threat to Jim Crow and racial subordination," reports the Equal Justice Initiative. "One of the principal elements causing concern is the returned Negro soldier who is not readily fitting back into his prior status of pre-war times. As bloodshed spread nationally veterans continued to be targeted. At least thirteen veterans were lynched across the United States after the war . . . in uniform which, when worn in public, many white people saw as an affront to America's racial caste system."[30]

Exemplary of the propaganda and mindset of the times was *Birth of a Nation,* a racist movie by D.W. Griffiths, inspired by the novel *The Clansman.* The 1915 classic depicted a racist and stereotypical portrait of Black people while glorifying the brutality of the Ku Klux Klan. The movie portrayed the Klan as the protector for the South and of white women; however, in reality, it was a terrorist organization that murdered thousands of Black people and assaulted and raped Black women.[31]

Over a million African Americans courageously served in the military during World War I, albeit in segregated units, and were amazed to be treated equitably by white Europeans in Germany, France, and the United Kingdom. These Black soldiers, with honorable discharges for sacrifices in defense of their country, were devastated to return home to the expectation that they resume their prior status of the Jim Crow South, with its overt bigotry and racism. Some soldiers who survived the war died at the hands of their white oppressors upon their return home.[32]

Washington, D.C. had an established Black middle class that in many ways symbolized its slow but expanding economic and social advances. After the Great Migration, they made up a quarter of the population. They also held jobs in the federal government and Industrial Savings, the country's earliest Black-owned bank. It was a steady march forward that white people needed to be halted.

Although not limited to veterans, white servicemen initiated racist attacks focused upon Black veterans. Recently returned white sailors on a days-long drunken rampage assaulted and lynched Black people on the Capitol's streets. "I knew it to be true, but it was almost an impossibility for me to realize as a truth that men and women of my race were being mobbed, chased, dragged from streetcars, beaten and killed within the shadow of the dome of the Capitol, at the very front door of the White House," wrote James Weldon Johnson, who coined the term "Red Summer" in *Crisis Magazine*. One Washington newspaper reported that the city had "passed through its wildest and bloodiest night since Civil War times."[33]

The situation escalated, but President Wilson refused to act. He was cultivating the perception of the United States as a global paragon of justice and was concerned that the riots would tarnish that image. He also had a demonstrated record of racism, including tacit support of the Ku Klux Klan.

Washington, D.C. had 5,000 Black veterans and self-defense was their last resort to decades of government in-action. After four days of anti-Black mob violence, 2,000 federal troops were deployed in Washington, D.C. to quell the riot. Across the country, former soldiers used their government-provided weapons training to defend their neighborhoods against vicious white mobs.

"When the riot explodes it's not so much some kind of a spontaneous event as it is a culmination. Black people [formed] ad hoc self-defense organizations to try to keep white folks from terrorizing their communities," said Simon Balto, professor of African American History at The University of Iowa. "Black veterans are instrumental in that." [34]

Before the war, the NAACP had 9,000 members. By the early 1920s, it had 100,000, indicating a growing boldness and cohesion to organizing that would eventually evolve into the Civil Rights Movement. [35]

Organized white violence against Blacks continued into the 1920s. In 1921 a white mob leveled Tulsa's "Black Wall Street," and in 1923 another one razed the [B]lack town of Rosewood, Florida. No one was punished. [36]

Racial lynchings of Black men, women, and children increased during this period. Hundreds of Black people were lynched, their tortured bodies dangling from trees. Billie Holiday, the jazz singer who grew up during this period, sang "*Strange Fruit.*" [37]

Southern trees bear a strange fruit
Blood on the leaves and blood at the root
Black bodies swinging in the Southern breeze
Strange fruit hanging from the Poplar trees.

Pastoral scene of the gallant South
The bulging eyes and the twisted mouth
Scent of the magnolia sweet and fresh
Then the sudden smell of burning flesh.

Here is a fruit for the crows to pluck
For the rain to gather for the wind to suck
For the sun to rot for the tree to drop
Here is a strange and bitter crop.

"Black Wall Street" Race Massacre, Tulsa, Oklahoma. At the turn of the 20th century, wealthy Black landowner O.W. Gurley left Arkansas and began opening businesses for Black residents, founding and developing the Greenwood district in Tulsa, Oklahoma, an all-Black community so wealthy that philosopher Booker T. Washington called it "Negro Wall Street." "Segregation kept Africa-Americans from patronizing white-owned shops, and Greenwood thrived from community support of Black-owned businesses."[38] Built on what had formerly been Indian Territory, the community grew and flourished as a Black economic and cultural mecca of nearly 10,000, with grocery stores, restaurants, hotels, theaters, and transportation services run by Black entrepreneurs, until May 31, 1921.

In one of the most horrific acts of racial carnage and domestic terrorism ever committed on American soil, a white mob began a rampage lasting 48 hours and decimating the Black community of Greenwood. "Members of the mob ransacked homes and stole money and jewelry. They set fires, 'house by house, block by block ... White pilots flew airplanes that dropped dynamite over the neighborhood,' making the Tulsa aerial attack among the first of an American city, according to the Commission Report."[39] When it was over, the city took surviving Black people to makeshift concentration camps. More than 1,200 businesses were destroyed, including a Black hospital, school, library, theatres, and banks. The frenzied throng of white people burned churches.[40] With a death toll of as many as 300, over 8,000 people were left homeless as their thriving Black community was burned to the ground. "Bodies of those killed would be stacked and discarded in mass graves and a river."[41]

"Survivors witnessed white men and women descending on Greenwood, killing Black people indiscriminately in what appeared to be ethnic cleansing. Occupied houses of Black people were set on fire. When the occupants ran out, members of the white mob shot them. Elderly Black people were shot as they kneeled in prayer. Black women and children were killed in the streets. Black men, with their hands held up in surrender, were shot dead by whites.[42] "Tulsa police took no action to prevent the massacre .... Reports indicate that some police actively participated in the violence and looting. The city deputized white civilians to shoot Black people. No one was ever prosecuted or punished for the violent criminal acts," concluded Human Rights Watch in a June 2021 report.[43] Yet Black Tulsans were indicted for inciting the riot.

After the event, city institutions destroyed documentation and spent 50 years pretending that nothing had happened. Officials began erasing it from the city's historical archive. Victims were buried in unmarked graves while police records vanished. For decades the event remained willfully buried. Tulsan Scott Ellsworth wrote a full history of the massacre, *Death in a Promised Land*, in 1982. City officials cleansed the history books so well that when attorney Nancy Feldman began teaching her students about the massacre at the University of Tulsa, they didn't believe her. State Senator Kevin Matthews said that despite being a Black person raised in Tulsa and the grandson of a woman survivor, he did not learn about the massacre until he was in his twenties.[44]

"In May 2021, 100 years after the massacre, 107-year-old Viola Fletcher testified before Congress: On May 31, of '21, I went to bed in my family's home in Greenwood. The neighborhood I fell asleep in that night was rich, not just in terms of wealth, but in culture . . . and heritage. My family had a beautiful home. We had great neighbors. I had friends to play with. I felt safe. I had everything a child could need. I had a bright future.

"Then, she said, came the murderous rampage, still vivid in her mind 100 years later: I still see Black men being shot, Black bodies lying in the street. I still smell smoke and see fire. I still see Black businesses being burned. I still hear airplanes flying overhead. I hear the screams." [45]

On June 1, a white mob descended into Greenwood and opened fire, some with machine guns, shooting Black people on sight, looting valuables, and setting buildings on fire, with occupants still inside. The mob stopped firefighters from entering, police and National Guard arrested Black citizens instead of the white rioters. Some Guard members joined the rioters.[46]

"The destruction of property is only one piece of the financial devastation that the massacre wrought. Much bigger is a sobering kind of inheritance: the incalculable and enduring loss of what could have been, and the generational wealth that might have shaped and secured the fortunes of Black children and grandchildren." [47] Tulsa stole millions of dollars from Black businesses and generational wealth. "Ongoing racial segregation, discriminatory policies, and structural racism have left Black Tulsans, particularly those living in North Tulsa, with a lower quality of life and fewer opportunities." [48]

Every Wednesday before night Bible study, Reverend Robert Turner appears in front of Tulsa's City Hall. He is the pastor of Vernon AME, the church that was burned on the main street in Greenwood. Black people fleeing the raging white mobs hid in the church's basement, one of the few remaining original structures that survived the massacre. He picks up his bullhorn as people gather to listen:

"Black people were murdered in this city, killed by mass racial terror," Turner shouts into a bullhorn. "Innocent lives were taken. Babies burned. Women burned. Mothers burned. Grandmothers burned. Grandfathers burned. Husbands burned. Houses burned. Schools burned. Hospitals burned. Our sanctuary burned. The blood of those you killed in Tulsa still cries out.

"These Black people asked for nothing from this city, state, or country. These former veterans from World War I came here and wanted to live out the American dream.

"Tulsa, how did you repay them? You, out of jealousy, out of racism, you went down to Greenwood and looted and killed innocent people and you dumped their bodies into mass graves.

"You know the first time bombs were dropped on American soil?" Turner demands. "The first time bombs were dropped on American soil was not during Pearl Harbor. The first time bombs were dropped on American soil was right here in Tulsa. You burned it to the ground and to this day, not one perpetrator has been charged with one crime.

"Until this day, the bodies of those who were slain are lying in unmarked graves.

"You made laws to prevent them from building homes and businesses back. What kind of civilized society burns churches?

"The blood of those you killed, the blood of those you killed in cold blood, in broad daylight. Their blood is on your hands." [49]

A History of Medical Abuse of African Americans. "Black Americans were kidnapped, raped, tortured, imprisoned and murdered as a matter of course. Segregation of [B]lack Americans was a legal status that tolerated the existence of [B]lack people but ensured white supremacy reigned over their lives generation after generation. Secret medical experiments were performed, eugenics experiments were authorized and funded by the federal government, states designed their own destructive measures to impact [B]lack lives," wrote author Mike Green. [50]

The United States Public Health Service conducted a clinical study from 1932-1972 called the Tuskegee Syphilis Study, also known as the Tuskegee Syphilis Experiment on African American Males, on 399 African American male sharecroppers, from Macon County, Alabama.

Many participants were deceived and given placebo treatments so that researchers could observe the entire long-term progression of the fatal disease. By the end of the study in 1974, only 74 of the original 399 were still alive, 28 of the men died of syphilis, 100 died of related complications, and 40 of the recorded wives had been infected. In addition, 19 of their children were born with congenital syphilis. This study was the longest non-therapeutic experiment on human beings in American medical history.[51]

In the 1950s, a woman named Henrietta Lacks was treated in the colored ward of Johns Hopkins Hospital for an overlooked, therefore undiagnosed, cancer. Doctors subjected her to aggressive radiation treatments, literally charring her body, but were unable to halt the cancer. Physicians removed tissue without her knowledge. Her rapidly replicating cells, the earliest human cells grown in culture, are still alive today. HeLa cells have been bought and sold by the millions, used in medical research internationally for the development of the polio vaccine, cancers, viruses, atom bomb effects, in vitro fertilization, cloning, and gene-mapping.

Although the sale of her cells launched a multi-million dollar industry, Henrietta Lacks is unknown, buried in an un-marked grave. Her family received no compensation, could not afford health insurance, and only learned of these "im-mortal" cells decades after her death, when scientists study-ing HeLa began using her husband and children in research without their consent.[52]

Given the Tuskegee Syphilis Study, the brutality of Jim Crow forced sterilizations in the Mississippi Delta, nick-named the "Mississippi appendectomy," African Americans and other people of color are disinclined to cooperate with the government because of its history of health misinforma-tion, medical, and testing abuses of minorities.

In 2020, America anxiously awaited the development and distribution of Coronavirus vaccines. The third and final testing stage required 30,000 *diverse* participants to determine a vaccine's utility. The resistance to Covid-19 vaccines reflected the lack of trust and credibility of public health and medical institutions, plus the recognition that many targeted minority and ethnically non-white international populations had not been tested for safety and efficacy. Institutional racism has far-reaching consequences and a prolonged memory of abuse and distrust.

The Poor People's Campaign. Dr. Martin Luther King Jr. was the spiritual leader and conscience of the Civil Rights Movement, progenitor of civil unrest with a non-violent creed. These movements appeared to address racial and gender bias in the country yet divided the nation by more than just the color line. Dr. King was committed to the fight for racial justice in America but was savvy enough to realize that civil unrest could appear as a divisive strategy to the white majority. He also believed that continuing exclusion and discrimination would ultimately result in an adverse effect. He affirmed this belief by his prophetic vision, "If we are not careful, our colleges will produce a group of close-minded, unscientific, illogical propagandists, consumed with immoral acts." [53]

In 1967, Dr King and the Southern Christian Leadership Conference (SCLC) established the "Poor People's Campaign: A National Call for Moral Revival," which was to be inclusive of race, gender, ethnicity, color, religion, sexual orientation and national origin, a movement to address systemic inequities for poor people. This period of civil unrest and despondency in America resulted in a violent tailspin with the assassinations of President John F. Kennedy on November 22, 1963; Dr. Martin Luther King Jr. on April 4, 1968; and Robert F. Kennedy on June 5, 1968.

Reparations for Descendants of Slavery. In addition to the absence of social equality, systemic racism has resulted in generational inequities in health, education, employment, housing, and finance.

The 2016 Brookings Institute report identified that the average net worth of a white family of three was twenty times that of a Black family of three. The Reparations Initiative has been championed in some states, North Carolina, Rhode Island, and California, to fund programs promoting business and career opportunities, and increased homeownership for their Black residents. [54]

For over 25 years, Detroit Congressman John Conyers, Jr. opened every session of Congress by introducing H.R. 40, a bill calling for a congressional study of slavery. The Commission to Study and Develop Reparation Proposals for African-Americans Act, introduced in the House on January 3, 2019, mandates examining slavery and discrimination in the colonies and the United States from 1619 to the present and recommending appropriate remedies. Among other requirements, the commission will identify (1) the role of the federal and state governments in supporting the institution of slavery, (2) forms of discrimination in the public and private sectors against freed slaves and their descendants, and (3) lingering negative effects of slavery on living African-Americans and society. No Republications supported the bill. [55]

Bruce's Beach Lodge offered a refuge for Black patrons in 1912 California's Jim Crow era. "There weren't many areas where Black people could get into the water along the entire coast of California at that time. [Bruce's Beach] was a place where people could have social functions. You had Black entertainers, actors and actresses, jazz artists, Black politicians as well as business owners and socialites," said Duane Shepard, descendant and representative of the Bruce family.

Black landowners have faced intimidation, violence, unjust property laws and extra-legal maneuvers such as eminent domain abuse for generations. The Bruces were harassed by their white neighbors and run out of Manhattan Beach, California; their property seized by the city, the resort shuttered, demolished, then abandoned for decades; and they lost their fortune.

Property law scholar Thomas W. Mitchell and the Land Loss and Reparations Research Project arrived at a preliminary estimate of a $300 billion loss on agricultural land alone unjustly stolen from Black farmers over the last hundred years. He estimated total loss of generational wealth for Black Americans across the United States into the trillions.

In September 2021, California's governor signed a bill authorizing the land transfer back to the Bruce family after nearly 100 years. "One of the reasons why the Bruce's case has been generating so much attention is because it represents the first instance in the history of the United States where an African American family or community that had their property taken unjustly, ended up having it returned," said Mitchell. The government stepped in to make amends for a historical wrong.[56]

In October 2021, the Department of Justice (DOJ) and the FBI agreed to an $88 million settlement for the survivors of the 2015 South Carolina Mother Emanuel AME church shooting and the families of the nine victims murdered by convicted white supremacist, Dylann Roof, who was sentenced to death in 2017. Roof's motive in killing the nine Black women and men during evening prayer was to start a race war.

The FBI was negligent in performing the background check on Roof, who had just turned 21 and was facing a narcotics charge. Due to the "Charleston loophole" (Gun sellers can sell firearms after three days regardless of whether the FBI's background check has been completed. If a buyer faces criminal charges, the gun store must deny the sale.), Roof was able to buy a .45 caliber Glock handgun with his birthday money. "A failure of the government to complete the gun check in three days is in effect a permission to the gun dealer to go ahead and complete the transaction (the sale)," argued Attorney William Wilkins.

Attorney Bakari Sellers said, "The settlement represents one of the largest settlements in a collection of civil rights cases in the nation's history. The $88 million figure is important beyond its high amount, because it represents a number special to white supremacists [H is the eighth letter of the alphabet, thus *"Heil Hitler"*], and Roof wore shoes with the number 88 on them." The settlement is a rebuke to "the white supremacists and racists in this country by saying we are taking this tragedy that they tried to tear this country apart with and [instead] build Black communities and generational wealth." Attorney Carl Pierce said, "This is about more than money. . . . This is about justice for the victims of gun and racial violence. The settlement also reflects a realization that the government has an important role to play in the responsible sale of guns."[57]

An Example from our German Ally. The term *Vergangenheitsbewältigung,* which translates to "coping with the past," describes the way Germany confesses and confronts its history. On the 50th anniversary of the liberation of the Auschwitz concentration camp, January 27, 1995, many

Germans dedicated the day to remember the Holocaust. A decade later the United Nations officially designated January 27th as International Holocaust Memorial Day.

The Memorial to the Murdered Jews of Europe, commissioned by the German parliament, opened in 2005. Beneath the memorial is The Room of Names with biographies of Jews murdered in the Holocaust. Gunter Demnig's *Stolpersteine*, or "stumbling blocks," commemorates victims on cobble stone-sized brass plates inscribed with their names, installed in the pavement of their last known residence. These and other commemorations concede their horror and apologize to their citizens and the world so they will never forget the gruesome reminders of a road never again to be traveled. Germany has provided a model for America by paying reparations of $40 billion to descendants of the Holocaust.[58]

CHAPTER 3

The Melting Pot Myth, America's Mandate of Assimilation

*T*he United States of America may well be a beacon for democracy to some, but it is not a model of equal opportunity for all. America, minus its Indigenous natives, was initially populated by the British and their landed gentry. After the Revolution of 1776 and the declaration of a new nation free from Britain, the United States inherited a society of former British descendants. The land of opportunity beckoned an influx of immigrants to a new free world. The primarily Western European diaspora, coupled with the need for them to fit into a single homogeneous society, resulted in an assimilation process known as "The Melting Pot."

It is important to note that the metaphor of the Melting Pot can represent two different societies: (1) an existing multicultural, heterogeneous society which will necessarily self-dilute over generations, becoming a more homogeneous population "melting together" into a less visibly diverse common culture; or (2) a monocultural society which enforces rigid assimilation, such that an influx of diversity and multiculturalism remains foreign, and its disparate cultural backgrounds threaten the homogeneity of the preexisting society, resulting in strife and disharmony.[1] America represents the latter.

Despite being Western European-based, the American Melting Pot process essentially required the shedding of one's nation-of-origin culture and the adherence to a British

American monoculture. It did not allow for cultural diversity, instead mandating assimilation into a fundamentally Anglo Christian society, with the singular language of English required for communication and acceptance.

Differences in language, religion, and cultural traditions were not tolerated. All new immigrants, Irish, Italians, Spanish, Jewish, were required to live in separate neighborhoods and to limit their ethnic and cultural differences to those communities. Since their cultures had similar values, the importance of family, deference to the elderly, honesty, empathy, and adherence to the belief that the group is more important than the individual, these isolating sacrifices for the sake of becoming American were tolerated.

Because they were all of European heritage, early immigrants appeared physically similar. Failure of the Melting Pot process of assimilation to address and accommodate diversity became apparent when non-European populations of Chinese, Japanese, Middle Eastern, and North Africans began to immigrate to America, and their physical differences could not be disguised.

America embodies two diametrically opposed definitions of a Melting Pot with conflicting social implications and outcomes. Although outwardly recognizing cultural diversity as a social, economic, and political reality of the 21st Century, it has spent 200 years downplaying its importance, instead enforcing the original Melting Pot assimilation to an American culture that has reached its natural end. We are awakening to cultural diversity with an appreciation and celebration of the enrichments it contributes. American society today is an intricate, energetic, and beautiful mosaic, no longer the static monoculture reflected in early Norman Rockwell paintings.

Immigration: Exemplars of Societal Exclusions

In January 1892, the United States established an Immigration Station at Ellis Island. Enter Annie Moore, a teenager from Ireland whose history symbolized America's past from the start. Ireland was the earliest English frontier before the colonization of America. The Irish were called "savages" by the English, their past foreshadowing the Native American future.[2]

The Irish came to America about the same time as the Chinese, with the distinct advantage of the Naturalization Act of 1790 allowing citizenship to "whites: only." They were seen as "the pioneers of the America urban ghetto," previewing experiences to be endured by Italians, Poles, and other groups from southern and eastern Europe. They developed an ethnic strategy, promoting Irish solidarity to garner political power and to eventually dominate blue-collar occupations, often at the expense of the Chinese and Blacks.[3] Annie Moore was followed by twelve million individuals between 1892 and November 1954, when Ellis Island finally closed its doors.

Congress passed The Naturalization Act of 1790, which allowed any free white person of good character living in the United States for two years or longer to apply for United States citizenship. Without citizenship, non-white residents, even those born in the United States, were denied basic constitutional provisions and protections, including the right to vote, own property, or testify in court.

The Asian Exclusion Act of 1875 began a progression of exclusions for people of color, explicitly identifying the terminology of exclusion. Next came the Chinese Exclusion Act of 1882 prohibiting all immigration of Chinese laborers. The Chinese Exclusion Act was the only law to have been implemented to prevent members of a specific ethnic or national group from immigrating to the United States. A long history of exclusionary events precede our contemporary version of inequity and discrimination by race and national origin.

No status of "illegal immigrant" existed until the Alien Registration Act of 1940 introduced Form AR-3, the initial version of the Green Card. This immigration document was required to enter the United States legally. Without these documents, or temporary visas, individuals were considered undocumented, or "illegal aliens." [4]

* * * * *

A daily reality of life in America for non-European and non-white citizens is that they are often assumed to be, and treated as, non-citizens. Many white Americans perceive exclusion and discrimination as elements of the past, even ancient history, but that is not the case. Although Muslims lived in America before there was an English colony at Jamestown,[5] before the United States of America, two groups targeted by racism in America since September 11, 2001 are the Arab and Muslim communities, who are learning that their acceptance here, even with citizenship, is not guaranteed, instead conditional.

Individuals with Arab and Muslim appearances and wardrobes have been accosted in public venues with hateful comments and physical assaults. Some have been removed from airplanes because of complaints and fears from white passengers, thus continuing the cycle of discrimination, unequal treatment of individuals due to negatively perceived group characteristics, and presumed dangerous group affiliations.

"Where [is] the public outrage over the more than 1,400 Arab, Arab Americans, Middle Easterners, and other "nonwhites" being detained without regard to their civil rights? How critical [are] we . . . to the steady flow of legislation being passed in the name of "homeland security" that violates our basic civil rights?"[6]

Governmental restrictions notwithstanding, this nation was built by immigrants, who, to this day, continue to contribute to our status as one of the most creative and productive societies in the world. Immigration begets innovation.

To value diversity is to appreciate differences, yet America has always preferred similarity and homogeneity, rejecting cultural and physical differences. We are challenged to advance along the cross-cultural continuum from ethnocentrism to multiculturalism.

What can trigger the drastic need to modify our current belief system and address the rejected notion that differences are value-laden? It was simply a matter of time before excluded populations would begin to question and challenge the incongruence of philosophies, procedures, and requirements for participation and inclusion. There is no reasonable cause for the disparity of treatment and participation, yet the inequities are undeniable. Opportunities for education, employment, economics, and housing are not equal, as promised. Few manage to break through barriers successfully. Those few then become misrepresented as stellar examples of equality.

An example of the benefit and utility of diversity and immigration as the world raced to produce vaccines for Coronavirus was Moderna, an American biotechnology company that created an mRNA vaccine, founded by Armenian refugee from Beirut Noubar Afeyan.[7] Immigration is a gateway to intellectual expertise and technological innovation from which America has reaped the benefits for generations.

Many non-white citizens such as Afeyan desperately wish to be seen, accepted, and respected as Americans rather than being categorized and judged on their visible nation-of-origin appearances, invalidated and treated as perpetual foreigners.

Chinese Immigrants

Asian Americans arrived before many European immigrant groups. However, as strangers from a different shore, they were stereotyped as heathen, exotic, and unassimilable. How the Chinese were treated set a precedent for the reception of the Japanese, Koreans, Filipinos, Asian Indians, and Southeast Asian refugees such as the Vietnamese and the Hmong.[8]

Almost thirty thousand men from southern China's poverty-stricken Guangdong Province made their hopeful treks to *Gum Saan,* Gold Mountain, at the start of the California Gold Rush in 1849. When the immigrants arrived in California, they found that the gold mountain was an illusion. Mining was unpredictable, goldfields were littered with disappointed prospectors, and locals were hostile.

Work was scarce and new arrivals sometimes found it challenging to earn enough to eat, let alone to strike it rich. They were cut off from their families. With no money, immigrants could not afford to bring family from China, or return home themselves. These men were stranded in a strange land far from home, one that did not welcome them, offered few means of survival, and in which they were very much alone.

In the middle of the nineteenth century, railroad companies were expanding at a breakneck pace, straining to span the continent as quickly and cheaply as they could.

The work was brutal, pay was subsistence, and workers were injured and killed at a very high rate. It represented an opportunity to enter the workforce for Chinese laborers, as they accepted lower wages than native-born American workers demanded.

More than ten thousand Chinese workers blasted tunnels, built roadbeds, and laid hundreds of miles of track in freezing cold or searing heat for the Central Pacific Railroad. Although the railroad could never have been completed in the record-breaking five years of construction without the toil of Chinese railwaymen, many of whom lost their lives along its route, few Chinese workers appeared in photographs when the final spike was driven into the rails of the Transcontinental Railroad in 1869.[9]

Since language barriers and racial discrimination barred them from established trades, Chinese immigrants operated shops, restaurants, produce stands, herb stores, and laundries in the growing mining towns of California. They also developed the farmland of the American West, including the plantations of Hawaii and the vineyards of California until 1882, when federal law halted their immigration.

With the onset of hard economic times in the 1870s, European immigrants and white Americans began to compete for the jobs traditionally held by the Chinese. With economic competition came distrust, racial suspicion, and hatred expressed in cruel racial epithets, violent anti-Chinese riots, mass lynchings, and pressure, especially in California, for the exclusion of Chinese immigrants altogether from the United States. This pressure resulted in the Chinese Exclusion Act of 1882 prohibiting the entry of immigrants based on nationality and ending Chinese immigration for nearly a century.[10]

Japanese Immigrants

After the Meiji Restoration in 1868, Japan's rapid urbanization and industrialization resulted in social disruption and agricultural decline. Migrant workers from Japan traveled to Hawaii, the *gannen mono* or "first-year people." [11]

In 1882, when Congress passed the Chinese Exclusion Act, the sugar planters of Hawaii had already begun to seek other cheap labor to replace their Chinese workers. The Japanese government signed a formal immigration agreement with the kingdom of Hawaii in 1885. During the next nine years, nearly thirty thousand Japanese crossed the ocean to work under three-year contracts for wages of $12.50 per month. Most were poor tenant farmers from the bottom economic strata in Japan. Unlike the *gannen mono,* these Japanese contract workers were accustomed to working in the fields. Seeing that the Japanese worked as strenuously as the Chinese, plantation owners soon competed to hire them. Plantation managers ordered the procurement of Japanese workers in the same memoranda in which they ordered macaroni, rice, horses, and mules. [12]

The Japanese government supported the contract labor system as a way of earning foreign exchange. Money remitted by the immigrants to Japan during the Meiji period amounted to more than two million yen annually. For a Japan struggling under foreign debts incurred to procure military equipment and other foreign goods, the foreign currency sent home by the immigrants was not an insignificant sum. [13]

The early 1900s began a twenty-five-year surge of immigration, more than 100,000 Japanese nationals. They were hired as migratory labor working the farms, mines, canneries, and railroads of the American West. Some became active in the labor agitation of the period. They also started businesses serving the needs of their community with Japanese restaurants, boarding houses, and shops, then department stores and tailoring chains catering to the general public. Japanese Associations provided financial support and advice. Using the labor-intensive growing methods of their homeland, many Japanese farmers were able to buy land and launch successful agricultural businesses, from farms to produce shops.

In 1908, the Japanese and American governments came to a "Gentlemen's Agreement." Japan limited emigration and the U.S. granted admission to families of immigrants already resident. Five years later the California legislature passed the Alien Land Law declaring all Asian immigrants "aliens," ineligible for citizenship, and from owning land in California, even land they had purchased years before.[14]

By 1920, Japanese immigrant farmers controlled more than 450,000 acres of land in California, brought to market more than 10 percent of its crop revenue, and had produced at least one American-made millionaire.[15]

Even at the peak of immigration, Japanese immigrants never made up more than a tiny percentage of the U.S. population. However, by the early years of the century, organized campaigns had already arisen to exclude Japanese immigrants from U.S. life. Sensational reports appeared in the English-language press portraying the Japanese as the enemies of the American worker, as a menace to American womanhood, and as corrupting agents in American society, repeating the same slanders used against Chinese immigrants in the decades before. The head of the American Federation of Labor, Samuel Gompers, denounced all Asians and barred them from membership in the nation's largest union. Legislators and mayors called for a Japanese exclusion act. Anti-Japanese legislation quickly followed.

Jewish Immigrants

Due to economic hardship, persecution, social and political upheavals of industrialization, overpopulation, and urbanization, millions of European Sephardic Jews left their towns and villages between 1820 and 1924, embarking on the arduous journey to the "Golden Land" of America.[16]

Early Jewish immigrants came mainly from Central Europe. A history of the Jewish upper-class in New York, prestigious names such as Loeb, Lehman, Lewisohn, Straus, Schiff, Seligman, Goldman, Warburg, and Guggenheim, a "citadel of privilege, power, and philanthropy" is presented by Stephen Birmingham in *Our Crowd, The Great Jewish Families of New York.* He tells us where they came from, how they made their money (Goldman, Sachs, Kuhn, Loeb, Lehman Brothers), and how they spent it (the Metropolitan Opera, the Museum of the City of New York, Lewisohn Stadium).[17]

Between 1881 and 1924 the migration shifted eastward, ejecting 2.5 million European Jews from their native lands, fleeing pogroms and religious persecution in Russia, followed by persecution and lack of economic opportunity in Europe. Most of these Ashkenazi immigrants settled in American cities, clustered in cramped districts close to downtowns, joined the working class, spoke Yiddish, and built strong networks of cultural, spiritual, voluntary, and social organizations. "Yiddish culture, in the form of drama, journalism, and prose, flourished in American Jewish immigrant neighborhoods, and the plight of the immigrant worker was a common cultural theme. The Eastern European Jews also brought with them certain ideological principles that would influence American Jewry. Many of the workers supported socialism or communism as a means of securing economic and social equality. In this manner, the Eastern Europeans established a strong link between American Jews and liberal politics."[18] This vision led Jews to struggle not only for themselves but also for other oppressed groups, especially Blacks.

After the 1917 East St. Louis race riot, Yiddish newspaper *The Forward* of New York compared the anti-Black violence to a 1903 pogrom in Russia, "Kishinev and St. Louis — the same soil, the same people." When Jackie Robinson broke into the Brooklyn Dodgers in 1947, Jews cheered. "He was adopted as the surrogate hero by many of us growing up at the time," recalled Jack Greenberg of the NAACP Legal Defense Fund. "He was the way we saw ourselves triumphing against the forces of bigotry and ignorance." Jews stood shoulder to shoulder with Blacks in the Civil Rights Movements. Two-thirds of the white volunteers who went south during the 1964 Freedom Summer were Jewish. The Jewish community is considered a highly successful ethnic group.[19]

Latinx Immigrants

Latin Americans have lived in North America since the 16th century. When the United States annexed Florida, Louisiana, and the northern half of Mexico in the early 1800s, more than 100,000 Spanish-speaking residents became American citizens. Most Latinx Americans in every decade since 1850 were born in the United States.

The United States invaded and conquered Mexico in 1847. They signed the Treaty of Guadalupe-Hidalgo in February 1848. Mexico forfeited what are now the states of California, Arizona, New Mexico, Colorado, and Utah, all appended to Texas, which had been surrendered a decade earlier.

In 1849 the California Gold Rush welcomed fortune seekers from around the world. By 1851 the rapidly growing

Anglo-American population had driven Latinx miners out of the gold country, some out of California altogether. Racism and violence toward Latinx grew as Anglo-Americans and Europeans expanded into the Southwest. The growing economy in the American West created jobs in agriculture and railroad construction resulting in a surge of immigrants from Mexico, disrupted only by the Great Depression. With job competition and xenophobia rising in many regions, some Latinx voluntarily left the United States.

However, needing workers in defense industries and agriculture during World War II, the U.S. government negotiated guest worker programs with Mexico and Caribbean colonies and countries. The Immigration and Nationality Act of 1965 established uniform national quotas and a variety of special statuses, making it challenging to obtain immigration visas, and dangerous to settle in the U.S. without them.[20]

1965-1970 the Delano Grape Farmworker Strike. On September 8, 1965 Filipino American grape workers, members of the Agricultural Workers Organizing Committee, walked out on strike against Delano-area table and wine grape growers protesting years of poor pay and conditions. The Filipinos asked Cesar Chavez, who led a mostly Latinx farmworkers union, the National Farm Workers Association, to join their strike.[21]

Chavez's union voted to join the Filipino worker's walkout on Mexican Independence Day, September 16, 1965, based upon the following agreement: (1) Latinx and Filipino strikers must work together, sharing the same picket lines, strike kitchens, and union hall. (2) Strikers must take a solemn vow to remain non-violent. (3) Strikers must commit not to quit until the strike was successful.

The strike drew unprecedented support beyond the Central Valley, from other unions, church activists, students, parents, community, and civil rights groups. The strike became known and supported globally.[22]

Chavez led a 300-mile march of 5,000 grape workers from Delano to Sacramento. It placed the plight of the farmworkers squarely before the conscience of the American people. The strikers turned to boycotts, including table grapes, which eventually spread across North America. The boycott connected middle-class families in big cities with poor farmworker families in the California vineyards. Millions stopped buying and eating grapes.[23]

Two and a half years into the strike, during the winter of 1967-68, some strikers, especially the young men, grew impatient. Some talked of violence toward the growers who abused them. In the tradition of his heroes Mahatma Ghandi and Dr. Martin Luther King Jr., Chavez was adamant about militant non-violence.

Chavez did not lecture or command. He led by example. In February 1968, Chavez announced a hunger strike to rededicate the movement to non-violence. He drank only water for 25 days. He lost 35 pounds. His doctors proclaimed his life in danger. All talk of violence stopped. Dr. King wrote Chavez expressing admiration and solidarity. The fast ended during a mass in Delano with thousands in attendance and support. Senator Robert F. Kennedy was present "out of respect for one of the heroic figures of our time." [24]

In 1970, table grape growers signed their union contracts granting workers better pay, benefits, and protections. These efforts continue to this day due to the unrecognized dedication and strength of Dolores Huerta,[25] the United Farm Workers Association, and the Cesar Chavez Foundation.

Huerta co-founded the United Farm Workers Association with Chavez and served as Vice-President of the United Farm Workers Union (UFW) until 1999.

Despite ethnic and gender bias, Huerta helped organize the 1965 Delano strike and was the lead negotiator in the workers' contract that followed, providing Aid for Dependent Families and Disability Insurance for farmworkers. Huerta fought for the dignity of farmworkers, resulting in the water and toilets now available in the fields. She coined the iconic phrase, *"Si se puede!,"* Yes we can!

She was inducted into the Women's Hall of Fame in 1993. President Barack Obama awarded Huerta the Presidential Medal of Freedom in 2012 and thanked her for allowing him use of her slogan during his campaigns. In 2014, President Obama proclaimed March 31 Cesar Chavez Day a federal holiday.

Four Elementary Schools in California, one Elementary School in Fort Worth, Texas, and a High School in Pueblo, Colorado, bear the name Dolores Huerta. In California, her birthday of April 10 is honored as Dolores Huerta Day. At 91 years old, she still leads the Dolores Huerta Foundation and works tirelessly developing leaders and advocating for the poor, women, and children.

Filipino Immigrants

October is Filipino American History Month. On October 18, 1587, Filipinos, or *"Luzon Indios"* landed in what is now the United States on a Spanish galleon near Morro Bay, California, about 33 years before Pilgrims from England arrived at Plymouth Rock.[26]

Migration from the Philippines to the United States was driven by longstanding political, military, and educational ties between the two countries, including a decades-long period of U.S. colonization. The Treaty of Paris ended the Spanish-American War in 1898. The signing of this treaty ignited the Philippine-American War, which ended in 1902 when the Philippine Organic Act was passed. The immigrants arrived when the Philippines became a United States territory, purchased from Spain for $20 million. The second wave of immigration spanned 1906 to 1935. They were predominantly *Sakadas*, low-wage laborers in California and Hawaii agriculture, Alaskan fish canneries, or *Pensionados*, wealthy students sponsored by the government and brought to Ivy League schools to enhance their education.[27]

During the 1920s and 1930s, sentiments became hostile and lawmakers amended anti-miscegenation laws to include Filipinos. The Tydings-McDuffy Act of 1935 granting the Philippines independence resulted in the reclassification of Filipinos as aliens, and limited immigration. In 1941 the United States began recruiting Filipino men to the military, promising citizenship. Thousands served in the Filipino 1st and 2nd Infantry Regiments, and in the Navy as stewards and cooks. World War II represented the third wave of immigration, military recruits and war brides. Many of these veterans eventually settled near military bases in the United States.[28]

After the 1965 Immigration Act, Filipinos fled the repressive political regime of President Ferdinand Marcos. Unlike earlier immigrants who were farmworkers and military personnel, the new wave of Filipino immigrants were highly-educated professionals, many in the medical fields (nurses, doctors, medical technologists), business people, engineers, and accountants. This fourth wave was the so-called "Brain Drain" generation of young educated professionals who arrived here in the 1960s.[29]

On September 8, 1965, Filipino American grape workers, members of the Agricultural Workers Organizing Committee, walked out on strike against Delano-area table and
wine grape growers protesting years of poor pay and conditions. The Filipinos asked Cesar Chavez, who led the National Farm Workers Association, to join their strike. (See the
Latinx Immigrants segment for the story.)

The Filipino immigrant population is the third-largest
foreign-born population from Asia, following India and China. Although dispersed across the nation, most Filipinos live
in California and Hawaii, where Filipino American History
Month is widely celebrated. In the San Francisco Bay Area,
where there is a significant Filipino American population,
both the San Francisco Giants baseball team and the Golden
State Warriors basketball team set aside one day in October
as Filipino American Day.

Korean, Vietnamese, and Hmong Refugees

Korean American history began in 1882 when the United
States signed a treaty of peace, friendship, and commerce
with Korea.

The Korean diaspora came in three waves. (1) From
1903–1905 about 7,500 Koreans, primarily men, became
contract laborers on Hawaii's sugar plantations. (2) From
1953–1989 approximately 300,000 "military brides," war
orphans, students, businessmen, and intellectuals arrived in
the United States. (3) The third wave began in 1967 when
Koreans came under the occupational and family reunifica-
tion provisions of the 1965 Immigration Act, "white collar"
workers settling in Los Angeles, New York, and Chicago.

Koreans were targets of anti-Asian violence and legislation. In 1913 Korean farmworkers were attacked by angry white workers who assumed they were Japanese. California passed the Alien Land Act in 1913, prohibiting Asians from buying property. Approximately 650 Koreans in Los Angeles County formed the South Central Los Angeles community during the 1930s. After the 1992 Los Angeles race riot, Koreans became committed to community empowerment and forging alliances with other minority groups.

In June 2002 the U.S. Senate passed a historic recognition of the 100th anniversary of Korean immigration to the United States. President George W. Bush recognized the centennial in January 2003, commending Korean Americans for their "important role in building, defending, and sustaining the United States of America."[30]

The Vietnam War, also referred to as the "American War in Vietnam," spanned 1954–1975. Approximately 123,000 refugees fled to the United States after the fall of Saigon in 1975. These generally high-skilled and well-educated individuals fearing reprisals for their close ties to Americans were airlifted out by the United States government. To prevent the formation of "ghettos," resettled Vietnamese were dispersed across the country. Many met hostility and racism due to the length and unpopularity of the war. However, the deliberate scattering of the initial influx was not successful, and most eventually moved to California and Texas.[31]

"Operation Babylift," the U.S. government plan to rescue orphans, transported over 3300 children out of war-torn Vietnam. More than 50,000 adults and families passed through the tent city of Camp Pendleton, California, many eventually settling in the Little Saigon district of Orange County. They were extremely grateful. "I remember grown men crying when they saw how the military cared for us and nurtured us," said Tony Lam, a former camp leader at Pendleton and first Vietnamese American elected to political office in the United States in 1992. Although the circumstances were very different, many felt a kinship with Central American refugees fleeing violence and other hardships.[32]

The second exodus out of Vietnam took place between 1978 and the mid-1980s, with almost two million refugees fleeing communist re-education camps and the 1979 Chinese invasion of Vietnam, asylum seekers in rickety wooden boats known as "Boat People." Many had been fishermen in Vietnam, so settled in fishing communities along the Texas Gulf Coast, finding work in low-paying jobs that local workers did not want. When they pooled their money to buy shrimp boats, competing with native-born locals and their fishing businesses, hostilities arose resulting in armed clashes with hooded Klu Klux Klan members.[33]

The United States engaged in a CIA-led ground operation in Laos from 1960–1975. Although not all Hmong joined the effort, they provided most of the manpower for the resistance. More than 200,000 Hmong refugees fled Laos. Due to our role in the war, approximately 90 percent of the refugees resettled in the United States, primarily in Minneapolis-St. Paul, Minnesota, Wisconsin, and Fresno, California. Approximately 3,500 soldiers and their families arrived in December 1975. The largest wave of Hmong immigrants came during the 1980s due to post-war hardships, declining economic conditions, crop failure due to ineffective communist farm schemes and drought, and repression of past and ongoing resistance activities. The final wave occurred during the summer of 2004 when the Thai monastery at Wat Tham Kabok closed its refugee complex in 2003 and the Laotian government refused to repatriate the Hmong because of their past resistance activities. They were resettled in Minnesota, Wisconsin, and California, joining relatives who arrived earlier.[34]

CHAPTER 4

Shikata Ga Nai, "It cannot be helped"

*H*ow do individuals from cultures all over the world survive punishing laws and governmental atrocities? It appears that to carry on in life, every ethnic or cultural group develops a meaningful way to accept and move on from unjust experiences.

One of the worst displays of American bigotry and racism occurred during the 1940s and World War II. As the war in Europe was escalating in 1941, Japan was invading Indo-China and Thailand. The United States retaliated by cutting off oil exports to Japan, while rising hostility resulted in anti-Japanese legislation at home. In America, Japanese Americans survived the bombing of Pearl Harbor by Japan, mandatory prison camps, and even fighting as American soldiers against their native homeland. Japanese immigrants and citizens were the only Americans since the Cherokee in 1838 to face wholesale forced removal from their homes, deprivation of their livelihoods, and mass incarceration.[1] In Japan, its citizens endured our atomic bombing of Hiroshima and Nagasaki.

Most Japanese immigrants to the United States arrived between 1885 and 1924. These nearly 160,000 migrants settled in California, Washington, and Oregon, with very few moving into the United States' interior. For example, in 1940, only eighteen Japanese Americans resided in Cleveland, Ohio.[2]

The prewar Japanese population of Chicago, Illinois numbered just under 400. Comprised of small business owners, service sector workers, and students, it differed markedly from its Pacific Coast contemporaries. Residentially they scattered throughout the city rather than concentrating in a segregated ethnic neighborhood. They did not encounter the widespread discrimination that their western agricultural counterparts faced. Also significant, Chicago was never subject to President Roosevelt's Executive Order 9066. This crucial exemption, along with an acute labor shortage and what the new government agency called the War Relocation Authority (WRA) described as a "comparative lack of anti-Oriental feeling," set the stage for wartime resettlement of the Japanese in the midwest.[3]

Agriculture engaged half of the Japanese population along the West Coast of California. Usually less than a quarter the size of typical California farms, the farms were tiny and often on substandard land, yet their yields were astonishing. Japanese Americans were master farmers using techniques handed down for generations. These farms were admired and coveted by their neighbors. Some believed the plan to remove families was a not-so-covert attempt to acquire their land. Japanese American farmers in California grew 95% of the state's strawberries and 33% of the state's truck crops. "We're charged with wanting to get rid of the Japanese for selfish reasons," said a representative of a California grower's association. "We might as well be honest. We do. It's a question of whether the white man lives on the Pacific Coast or the brown man." [4]

The massive attack on Pearl Harbor by Japanese aircraft on December 7, 1941, forced the United States into war against Japan. All American citizens of Japanese ancestry were immediately classified 4-C, or "enemy aliens." Under the FBI, local authorities began imprisoning the *Issei* leadership of Japanese American communities in Hawaii and the mainland.

Although the men were not formally charged, most spent the war years in camps, separated from their families.

The fishing village of Terminal Island, near a naval base, an airstrip, and the Port of Los Angeles shipyards, was a top security priority for the FBI. "The Terminal Islanders were perhaps more thoroughly victimized than any other group of Japanese Americans," the Department of the Interior reported in 1945. Residents were given a thirty-day evacuation notice but were required to leave within forty-eight hours. Their homes were bulldozed and fishing boats requisitioned by the Navy.[5]

Concentration Camps in America. The Japanese phrase "*Shikata ga nai*," which translates to "it cannot be helped" or "it must be done"[6] is a cultural explanation of why 120,000 Japanese, over 80,000 American-born citizens, did not riot or resist President Roosevelt's Executive Order 9066 in February 1942. They forfeited their possessions, livelihoods, everything they owned except what they wore and could carry onto buses or trains. They were relocated and interned without being charged a crime, a deprivation of due process under the law. Many sold businesses, homes, and farms to white Americans at significant losses. Historians estimate that Japanese Americans lost $350 million through these sales (the equivalent of more than $5 billion in 2018).[7]

Executive Order 9066 authorized military commanders to designate zones "from which any or all persons may be excluded, and with respect to which, the right of any person to enter, remain in, or leave shall be subject to whatever restrictions the Secretary of War or the appropriate Military Commander may impose in his discretion." Although not named in the text of the Executive Order, Japanese Americans were immediately incarcerated. The WRA was responsible for removing "enemy aliens" from these designated zones. They forcibly deported approximately 120,000 *Issei* and *Nisei* to ten isolated and desolate military areas prison camps in seven states:

(1) Topaz, Utah; (2) Poston, Arizona; (3) Gila, Arizona; (4) Amache, Colorado; (5) Heart Mountain, Colorado; (6) Jerome, Arkansas; (7) Manzanar, California; (8) Minidoka, Idaho; (9) Rohwer, Arkansas; and (10) Tule Lake, California, throughout the interior of the United States from 1942–1946.[8]

The *Issei* and *Nisei* were targeted because of their ancestry. The WRA detained only 14,000 "enemy aliens" born in Europe (most from Axis powers and wartime enemies of the United States, Germany and Italy) out of more than one million European immigrants living in the United States who were not yet U.S. citizens. Millions of Americans whose parents had immigrated from Europe were not forcibly removed, but the *Nisei* were.[9]

Fred Toyosaburo Korematsu. Not every Japanese American was cooperative and compliant. Fred Korematsu was publicly defiant of Executive Order 9066. When Japanese Americans were ordered to report to Assembly Centers for assignment to Internment Camps on May 9, 1942, Korematsu instead went into hiding. He was arrested three weeks later and held at a jail in San Francisco.

The American Civil Liberties Union in Northern California asked Korematsu whether he would be willing to use his case to test the legality of Executive Order 9066 for

Japanese Internment. Korematsu agreed, was tried, convicted in federal court in September 1942, transported directly from the courtroom to the Tanforan Assembly Center, and placed in a horse stall with a single light bulb, later commenting, "jail was better than this. These camps [are] definitely an imprisonment under armed guard with orders [to] shoot to kill. These people should have been given a fair trial in order that they may defend their loyalty at court in a democratic way." [10]

The Korematsus, a family of six adults, were then transported to the Topaz, Utah Internment Camp. His father scolded him for getting in trouble and his mother and brothers were ashamed he'd been arrested. He was viewed as a troublemaker, isolated and shunned by the other Japanese American residents. "Many *Nisei* believed that they would prove their patriotism by complying." [11]

Widely rejected but never overturned, legal scholars have long considered *Korematsu v. United States* as part of the anticanon, a collection of high-profile Supreme Court cases that were wrongly decided, alongside *Plessy v. Ferguson* and *Dred Scott v. Sandford*. The *Korematsu* ruling held that the executive order authorizing World War II-era Japanese-American incarceration was constitutional. *Plessy* upheld the constitutionality of segregation and *Dred Scott* held that people of African descent could not be U.S. citizens. [12]

In January 1944 Korematsu appealed to the U.S. Court of Appeals, which upheld the lower court's verdict. He then appealed to the United States Supreme Court. In December 1944, the Supreme Court held that compulsory exclusion, though constitutionally suspect, was justified during

circumstances of "emergency and peril," becoming the precedent for the establishment of the Homeland Security Act
after the Twin Towers bombing on September 11, 2001.

In November 1983, U.S. District Court in San Francisco
formally voided the decision. The ruling cleared Korematsu's
name but was incapable of overturning the Supreme Court's
decision. He told Judge Marilyn Patel that instead of a legal
pardon, he wanted to be assured the U.S. Government would
never again take such an action. Korematsu testified, "I would
like to see the government admit that they were wrong and
do something about it so this will never happen again to any
American citizen of any race, creed, or color." He added, "If
anyone should do any pardoning, I should be the one pardoning the government for what they did to the Japanese
American people." [13]

Korematsu became a civil rights activist lobbying Congress to pass the Civil Liberties Act of 1988, which gave
compensation and an apology to former wartime detainees.

President Bill Clinton awarded Korematsu the highest
civilian honor in the United States, the Presidential Medal of
Freedom, in 1998. The presidential citation issued with the
award read:

> In 1942, an ordinary American took an extra-
> ordinary stand. Fred Korematsu boldly opposed
> the forced internment of Japanese Americans
> during World War II. After being convicted for
> failing to report for evacuation, Mr. Korematsu
> took his case all the way to the Supreme Court.
> The high court ruled against him. But 39 years
> later, he had his conviction overturned in federal
> court, empowering tens of thousands of Japanese

Americans and giving him what he said he
wanted most of all—the chance to feel like
an American again. In the long history of our
country's constant search for justice, some
names of ordinary citizens stand for millions of
souls: Plessy, Brown, Parks. To that distinguished
list, today we add the name of Fred Korematsu.[14]

After the September 11, 2001 attack, Korematsu
demanded the government should not allow the same
treatment of Middle Eastern citizens that befell Japanese Americans in 1942. When prisoners were detained at
length in Guantanamo Bay, he filed amicus briefs with the
Supreme Court warning them not to repeat the mistakes
of the Japanese Internment.

Fred Korematsu died in March 2005 at the age of 86.
One of his final statements: "I'll never forget my government
treating me like this. And I really hope this will never happen
to anybody because of the way they look, if they look like the
enemy of our country." He also urged others to "protest, but
not with violence, and [not to be] afraid to speak up. One
person can make a difference, even if it takes forty years."[15]

Dale Minami, lead attorney on Korematsu's 1983 team,
said, "This was a case that involved a massive travesty of justice to a minority group ... who were denied basic due process, the right to a trial, the right to a notice of the charges,
the right to attorneys even. They were just summarily whisked
— banished essentially — to these prisons for indefinite confinement.... We thought that this was a chance to not only
correct history ... but also impair one of the worst precedents
ever composed by the Supreme Court," Minami added.[16]

In 2014, the late Justice Antonin Scalia denounced the decision in *Korematsu v. U.S.*, while issuing a warning to his audience of law students in Hawaii, "But you are kidding yourself if you think the same thing will not happen again. ...I would not be surprised to see it happen again, in time of war. It's no justification but it is the reality." [17]

While the convictions of Korematsu and others were overturned in the '80s, the Supreme Court did not formally repudiate the case until its 2018 ruling on the Trump [Muslim] travel ban in *Trump v. Hawaii*.[18] Supreme Court Chief Justice John Roberts condemned that decision, writing, "The forcible relocation of U.S. citizens to concentration camps, solely and explicitly on the basis of race is objectively unlawful and outside the scope of presidential authority. *Korematsu* was gravely wrong the day it was decided, has been overruled in the court of history, and—to be clear— 'has no place in law under the Constitution.'" [19]

Gordon Kiyoshi Hirabayashi, born in Seattle, Washington, was an American sociologist and conscientious objector to the Japanese American internment during World War II. He was one of the only individuals to challenge the curfew and removal orders being enforced against Japanese on the West Coast citing "Christian principles" and asserting "a duty to maintain the democratic standards for which this nation lives."

In preparing to come to the United States, his parents had two major objectives: learning English and being Christian. Hirabayashi's parents had become members of Mukyokai, the "non-church" movement in Japan. Teaching Christian principles free from denominational issues, Mukyokai stressed an uncompromising stand against social injustice.

Growing up on a farm outside of Seattle, he said, "while there were restrictions, and we knew we weren't equal, we learned to bend with the blows . . . which weren't serious except the Alien Land Law preventing landownership." Gordon Hirabayashi became a Quaker while a student at the University of Washington and was involved in social services. When he learned of Executive Order 9066, the concern was for his parents who were deemed "enemy aliens." The *Nisei* did not fear for themselves because "We're citizens. They can't do this to us." [20]

Hirabayashi also reflected that "Shortly after that curfew orders were imposed, which included all 'enemy aliens,' German, Italian and Japanese aliens, plus other persons of Japanese ancestry, that's me. And it's interesting, I never was included as a citizen. That is, they didn't say 'citizens of Japanese ancestry are also included,' they always referred to me as a 'non-alien.' If you look at the definition of 'alien' as being a 'non-citizen,' a 'non-alien' is a kind of a double negative. And they used that euphemism throughout the war. I, like any other normal American, trained to obey laws that were issued by the government or in the name of the government, I complied with the curfew. And I lived in a small dormitory right next to the campus, University of Washington, YMCA dormitory." [21]

Initially, Hirabayashi complied with the curfew, being the only Japanese American in his dormitory leaving his fellow students in the library while he returned home. By the end of the week it dawned on him that if he was an American, why was he dashing back and his friends not? He said it might have been a different experience if he lived in the Japanese Students Club where 150 people congregated during the day and about 40 lived at night. He felt that they would all be complaining but going home as a group, instead of sticking out like a sore thumb, as he did. He said, "Well, if I'm an American, I'm gonna act like one," turning around to return to the library instead of heading for his dorm.

Hirabayashi refused to comply with the curfew imposed on Japanese Americans in the wake of the attack on Pearl Harbor by failing to report for relocation to the internment camps because the directives were based solely on race and therefore unconstitutional. "I was asked questions by my lawyer as to why I did it, and what were my reasons. And my response was that I was trying to live like an American, and that I believed what the Constitution said, that being of Japanese ancestry should not constitute grounds for removal. If they suspected me of a threat to national defense, they should accuse me of that so I could defend myself on that ground, not on ancestry. If I gave in to this, it would cause me to change my ideals, my beliefs, my whole philosophy of life. I knew I'd be accused of disloyalty, but I couldn't sit back and passively endorse the orders. Ancestry is not a crime." [22]

Hirabayashi had a philosophy as an American. If he were to forsake those principles and accept second-class status, he would have to alter his entire life outlook. He decided to stick with his existing convictions, understanding that they would result in arrest and whatever followed. After the last Japanese were forcibly removed from Seattle, Hirabayashi stayed one day extra. That made him, according to authorities, present illegally. He turned himself in to the FBI and was tried and convicted in the Federal District Court of Seattle. (The case ultimately went to the Supreme Court, which ruled that the curfew was constitutional.) Hirabayashi was sentenced to serve three months in a minimum-security prison in Arizona.

No funds were available to transport him, so he spent two weeks hitchhiking to get there. He was then tried and convicted of draft resistance and served nine months in the federal prison on McNeil Island in Washington.

While imprisoned, Hirabayashi "followed basically the same principles in prison as I did outside. And when I was confronted with situations that I could not accept, I had to refuse it in prison, too. So I did make one conscientious effort in prison. I tried to distinguish between the acts that I . . . or the orders that I could not accept from those who were forced to issue those orders, and I tried to stay as friendly as possible with the officials, even if I refused the order. That wasn't always understood by them." [23] His logic, clarity, and defiance resulted in the integration of the previously all-white prison barracks, among other negotiations.

When released, Hirabayashi returned to the University of Washington and received BA, MA, and PhD degrees in sociology. He taught overseas at the American University in Beirut and the American University at Cairo. He retired as chair of the sociology department at the University of Alberta in 1983, and continued to speak out in defense of civil rights for the rest of his life.

Today those who turn up Prison Camp Road outside Tucson, Arizona, no longer find the federal camp where Hirabayashi was imprisoned. Instead they are greeted by a U.S. Forest Service plaque dedicating the *Gordon Hirabayashi Recreation Site* and panels introducing them to the history of the Japanese Americans during World War II. One quotation sums up his life's endeavor: "I was always able to hold my head up high because I wasn't just objecting and saying 'no,' but was saying 'yes' to a prior principle, the highest of principles." [24]

In May 2012, President Barack Obama conferred the Medal of Freedom on Gordon Hirabayashi; unfortunately, it was a posthumous honor (Hirabayashi had died earlier that year), with the medal accepted by his wife and children. In the citation issued for the ceremony, President Obama said:

> Gordon Hirabayashi knew what it was like to stand alone. As a student at the University of Washington, Gordon was one of only three Japanese Americans to defy the executive order that forced thousands of families to leave their homes, their jobs, and their civil rights behind and move to internment camps during World War II. He took his case all the way to the Supreme Court, and he lost. It would be another 40 years before that decision was reversed, giving Asian Americans everywhere a small measure of justice. In Gordon's words, 'It takes a lot of courage in the face of military power in the crisis to tell us that unless citizens are willing to stand up for the [Constitution], it's not worth the paper it's written on.' And this country is better off because of citizens like him who are willing to stand up.[25]

Unfinished Business: The Case for Supreme Court Repudiation of the Japanese American Internment Cases is an essay by Professor Peter Irons, who initiated and served as counsel to Fred Korematsu and Gordon Hirabayashi in their *coram nobis* actions to vacate their wartime internment convictions in 1982. The Supreme Court, in the Japanese American internment cases, turned a blind eye to the "grave injustice" imposed on this entire ethnic and racial minority, whose members were guilty of nothing more, as Fred Korematsu later told the federal judge who vacated his conviction, than "looking like the enemy."

"This essay presents the case for the Supreme Court to follow President Lincoln's example by formally repudiating its decisions in the Japanese American internment cases, issuing a public statement acknowledging that these decisions were based upon numerous and knowing acts of governmental misconduct before the Court, and were thus wrongly decided. These acts of misconduct, documented and discussed herein, were committed by several high-ranking military and civilian officials (including the Solicitor General of the United States) before and during the pendency of the internment cases before the Supreme Court. Consequently, the Court was forced to rely in making its decisions on records and arguments that were fabricated and fraudulent. Sadly, the Court's unquestioning acceptance of these tainted records, and its upholding of the criminal convictions of Gordon Hirabayashi, Minoru Yasui, and Fred Korematsu, has left a stain on the Court's integrity that requires the long overdue correction of public repudiation and apology, as both the legislative and executive branches of the federal government— to their credit—have now done." [26]

Over the past decades, many distinguished scholars and judges have implored the Court to repudiate the internment decisions. Perhaps most distinguished of these voices, Eugene V. Rostow, professor and dean at Yale Law School, published an article in the *Yale Law Journal* entitled "The Japanese American Cases — A Disaster."

His article eviscerated the Court's opinions as based on unsupported racial stereotypes and without the benefit of the evidence opinions, of governmental misconduct discussed above. Professor Rostow wrote that those "[b]y their acceptance of ethnic differences as a criterion for discrimination . . . are a breach, potentially a major breach, in the principle of equality. Unless repudiated, they may encourage devastating and unforeseen social and political conflicts." He continued: "In the political process of American life, these decisions were a negative and reactionary act. The Court avoided the risks of overruling the Government on an issue of war policy. But it weakened society's control over military authority—one of those polarizing forces on which the organization of our society depends. And it solemnly accepted and gave the prestige of its support to dangerous racial myths about a minority group, in arguments which can be applied easily to any other minority in our society." [27]

"[T]hat the Supreme Court has upheld imprisonment on such a basis constitutes an expansion of military discretion beyond the limit of tolerance in democratic society. It ignores the rights of citizenship, and the safeguards of trial practice which have been the historical attributes of liberty. . . . What are we to think of our own part in a program which violates every democratic social value, yet has been approved by the Congress, the President and the Supreme Court?" [28]

In 1945, Supreme Court Justice Owen J. Roberts wrote: "An Assembly Center was a euphemism for a prison. No person within such a center was permitted to leave except by Military Order." Decades later Justice Tom C. Clark, who was one of the architects of the incarceration, said "We picked them up and put them in concentration camps. That's the truth of the matter." [29]

Questions 27 & 28 and The No-No Boys. In 1943 every resident of the ten internment camps was required to answer two questionnaires, one misleadingly entitled "Application for Leave Clearance," each to determine loyalty. Question 27 asked if an individual would be willing to serve as a combat soldier, nurse, or Women's Army Auxiliary Corps. Question 28 was more complex: "Will you swear unqualified allegiance to the United States . . . and forswear any form of allegiance or obedience to the Japanese emperor, to any other foreign government, power or organization?" [30]

"Guilt by association" is a concept to label individuals guilty without proof of wrongdoing. Question 28 was precarious for the *Issei* Japanese, who were denied American citizenship based on race. If they declared Yes, they were no longer citizens of any country and essentially stateless.

Of 75,000 completed questionnaires, 6,700 answered No to Questions 27 and 28, whom the interned Japanese referred to as the No-No Boys. These individuals found it disingenuous for the government to demand loyalty without reciprocity. All No-No Boys were transported to the Tule Lake Internment Camp in California.

The Japanese American Citizens League (JACL), founded in 1929, is the oldest and largest Asian American non-profit organization committed to upholding the civil rights of Americans of Japanese Ancestry. [31] The JACL was essential in pressuring the U.S. government to admit the injustice of the internment of 120,000 Japanese Americans.

A challenge for the JACL was the internal conflict between the *Nisei* majority and the *Sansei* minority membership. The *Nisei* Japanese, the earliest generation to be born into U.S. citizenship, was a very conservative and traditional cultural group, while the *Sansei* was a more liberal and social activist group.

The discord created a rift among the JACL and a credibility clash among Japanese American organizers and lawyers. The *Nisei* JACL leadership and their followers condemned the No-No Boys as disloyal cowards, blaming them for making the American public think that Japanese Americans were unpatriotic. The *Sansei* vehemently disagreed, viewing the No-No Boys as heroes for standing up to a government that deprived them of their constitutional rights.

It took the *Sansei* children, most born in the Internment Camps, to reconcile the divisive positions on loyalty and the No-No Boys. Dale Minami, lead attorney in the resolution of the Fred Korematsu legal injustice, and other *Sansei* lawyers, strongly supported the JACL leadership in accepting the No-No Boys as a positive necessity in addressing the inequities of Executive Order 9066. They exposed the illegal government conduct of suppression and destruction of evidence, and the truth behind the unlawful incarceration of Japanese Americans, thereby closing the circle of shame.

The JACL accepted the rationale of pursuing the government for an apology and reparations as a constitutional issue rather than a solely Japanese American issue. They believed this was necessary to ensure this could never happen again to any other group of American citizens.

A more progressive organization was created to address the injustice, Nikkei for Civil Rights & Redress (NCRR), formerly known as the National Coalition for Redress and Reparations. NCRR supports Representative John Conyers (D-MI) H.R. 40, the bill to study proposals for reparations to African Americans. Erasures of the experiences of excluded people of color are counterproductive. Omitting injustice from documentation does not eradicate its existence.[32]

The 442nd Regiment. While the scope of their contribution to the war effort remained hidden for more than half a century, the *Nisei* soldiers were among the most courageous and successful soldiers of World War II. The Hawaiian and mainland *Nisei* trained together, despite their vastly different lifestyles and philosophies. While in military training in America's South, the Hawaiian *Nisei* were astonished to observe the mistreatment and resultant demeanor of Black citizens, despite their subservience to white owners under Hawaii's exploitative plantation system. They battled openly in their close quarters, the serious, hard-working, farming mainland *Nissei* unappreciative of their relaxed, ukelele-playing, pidgin-speaking, gambling, playful Hawaiian counterparts. Ultimately, the two factions forged themselves into a tight-knit camaraderie that would last a lifetime, and they deployed to Europe as a single "Go for Broke" 442nd unit, in spirit and deed.

The *Nisei* were uniquely equipped to fight for America. They embodied the Samurai's code of *Bushido*, rectitude, courage, benevolence, politeness, honesty, honor, loyalty, and self-control; *Yamato damashii*, the virtue of sticking together no matter what, fighting for your group rather than for yourself; and *ohana*, the Hawaiian concept of one another belonging to the same big family. They also received the same admonitions from their fathers: "Don't do anything that will bring shame to the family and the Japanese race. Do your best no matter what. Keep your self-dignity. . . . Be a good soldier. Come home alive if you can. But whatever you do, don't bring shame on yourself or your country or the family. . . . Whatever you do, don't bring shame on the family. . . . You chose your side. Now do it. If they tell you to go out and get shot, you go out and get shot."

It is no wonder that the 442nd was in high demand in combat missions, and perceived as "the little iron men" throughout Europe and in America's newspapers and newsreels. One veteran from Spokane, Washington, Fred Kisaburo, described himself, "a 6-foot, 8-inch lumberjack housed in a 5-foot, 6-inch body." [33]

The Hawaiian National Guard, comprised mainly of *Nisei* Japanese, was federalized and became the 100th Infantry Battalion. After *Nisei* eligibility for the draft was restored in 1944, 14,000 Japanese American men whose families were in concentration camps did sign Selective Service Form 304A "Statement of United States Citizens of Japanese Ancestry," and volunteered into the segregated 442nd Infantry Regiment Combat Unit, led by white commanders. The 522nd Field Artillery Battalion was an integral component of the 442nd Regimental Combat Team, with backgrounds in science and engineering, using their strong mathematical skills to make the necessary calculations for firing the guns and hitting their targets.

The 100th Infantry Battalion joined the 442nd Regimental Combat Team and fought together in Italy, France, and Germany, rescued the "Lost Battalion" (800 *Nisei* casualties to rescue 211 men from Texas), while the 522nd Field Artillery Battalion liberated the survivors of the Dachau death camp.

The 442nd Regiment was the most decorated unit for its size in United States military history, earning more than 18,000 awards in under two years: Distinguished Service Crosses, Silver Stars, Legion of Merit Medals, Bronze Star Medals, Commendation Medals, more than 4,000 Purple

Hearts, eight Presidential Unit Citations and twenty-one Medals of Honor.

In October 1963 Governor John Connally made the entire 442nd RCT honorary Texans.[34] In 2010, Congress approved granting the Congressional Gold Medal to the 442nd Regimental Combat Team. In 2012, all surviving members became *Chevaliers* of the French *Legion d'Honneur* for their actions contributing to the liberation of France and their heroic rescue of the Lost Battalion. Every year the French invite and honor all the surviving members of the Japanese American 442nd Regiment.[35]

As well, nearly 6000 additional *Nisei* soldiers served in the Military Intelligence Service, most of them in the Pacific theater of operation, fighting the Japanese imperial forces. Trained as translators, interrogators, propaganda writers, and radio announcers, many of them served behind the front lines, others embedded in active combat units in the jungles and on the beaches of the Philippines, Burma, New Guinea, and every other combat zone the U.S. troops fought in the Pacific.[36]

April 5 is celebrated as National "Go For Broke" Day, the motto of the 442nd RCT, in commemoration of PFC Sadao Munemori who was killed in action near Seravezza, Italy, and the earliest recipient awarded the Medal of Honor. A film *Go for Broke* was released in 1951. The "Go For Broke National Education Center," located in Los Angeles, California, features a hands-on participatory learning experience called the *Defining Courage Exhibition,* teaching the history of Japanese Americans in World War II and its relevance to our lives today.

Resettlement. When more workers and soldiers were needed, some of the internees were allowed to leave the camps. Many of these Japanese Americans found employment in Midwestern cities, as the federal government refused to allow return to their homes on the West Coast.[37] This period was an extraordinary moment in Japanese American history. *Issei* and *Nisei* "resettlers," or participants in the War Relocation Authority's ethnic dispersal program, accounted for a rapid and massive influx of thousands migrating to midwestern cities, cognizant of the federal government's imperative to "assimilate" into the white middle-class. Ultimately, resettlers collectively challenged the WRA's assimilationist vision and established a Japanese American community in Chicago.[38]

The WRA and its civilian partners imagined post-detention migration throughout the United States "resettlement" as a plan to refashion ethnic Japanese into model American citizens via state-engineered cultural and structural assimilation. They wanted *Issei* and *Nisei* to identify and associate entirely with mainstream America. As one Chicago resettlement coordinator explained, assimilation entailed "the complete incorporation or absorption into our every community social activity where only the difference in physical features are noticeable."[39]

Less than a third of the 36,000 prisoners participated in the resettlement program by the end of 1944, starting over throughout the Midwest, the East Coast, and the mountain states. Of these, 6,599 found their way to Chicago, the most popular destination in late 1942.

Chicago offered plentiful and diverse employment prospects without anti-Asian animus. Defense-related industries sought laborers, and resettlers eagerly applied for positions in munitions factories. Others took service-sector (domestic, restaurant, and hospitality), clerical, or light manufacturing jobs, with many gravitating towards large companies willing to take on Japanese resettlers *en masse*. Notably, many employers preferred *Issei* and *Nisei* employees as an alternative to hiring African Americans. Some resettlers became small business owners and professionals.[40]

The WRA and its partner organizations understood their mission was facilitating Japanese American integration, but they placed the onus of assimilation on the *Nisei* themselves. They repeatedly emphasized that resettlers should "avoid segregation at all costs" and "spread out thinly," joining *"Hakujin* [white]" groups, churches, clubs, and professional associations whenever possible.[41]

Racial discrimination impeded assimilation. Despite an absence of restrictive covenants aimed at the Japanese, locating housing was difficult for many resettlers. They were only able to rent apartments and homes in specific areas, zones of transition, or buffer regions between white and Blacks, on the city's Southside. Resettlers and other racial minorities, particularly African Americans, encountered racism in the workplace and public spaces such as dance halls, hospitals, and even cemeteries.[42]

Despite many Japanese Ohioans returning to their homes on the West Coast at the war's conclusion in 1945, Ohio's major cities saw a marked increase in their Japanese population. The number of Japanese in Cleveland soared to 3,500 by 1946.[43] Chicago became home to more than 20,000 by 1947.[44]

On December 17, 1944, Public Proclamation No. 21 declared that effective January 2, 1945, Japanese American "evacuees" from the West Coast could return to their homes. The announcement came one day before the Supreme Court granted Mitsuye Endo (the woman behind the landmark 1944 Supreme Court Case) her liberty from Topaz, Utah, because the Department of Justice and the WRA conceded that Endo was a "loyal and law-abiding citizen," and that no authority existed for detaining loyal citizens longer than necessary to separate the loyal from the disloyal. One of four "internment" cases, Endo's was the only one that resulted in a victory. Although born in Sacramento, California, she quietly resettled in Chicago, married, and had three children. Her own daughter did not learn of her mother's role in history until in her twenties.[45]

President Franklin Roosevelt opened the camps because he knew the Supreme Court decision was coming. He told reporters in November 1944, "There are roughly a hundred thousand Japanese-origin citizens in this country and it is felt by a great many lawyers that under the Constitution they can't be kept locked up in concentration camps."[46]

It took months to close down the camps; most stayed open through late 1945. Germany surrendered to end the war in Europe on May 7, 1945. The United States dropped an atomic bomb on Hiroshima on August 6, 1945. Three days later, it dropped a second atomic bomb on Nagasaki. World War II ended on August 14, 1945. At a press conference in 1975, Emperor Hirohito lamented the nuclear bombs and Hiroshima's loss of its citizens, "but it couldn't be helped because that happened in wartime." *Shikata ga nai.*

The Japanese experienced racism and overt hatred upon their release in 1945. After the WRA closed the camps, U.S. officials gave internees little financial or material support, simply forcing them to vacate the camps. Prisoners were given \$25 and a train ticket to *nowhere*, unable to return to their homes or communities. They were unprepared for the vitriol with which they were received. California didn't want the Japanese to return.[47]

Gordon Hirabayashi explained that the cooperation of the majority of Japanese Americans reflected Japanese culture and society and how they all learned to cope and survive in North America. They arrived as an alien group in a country most people considered white man's country. They still think that. "Other" peoples weren't humans that counted, so were simply ignored. Psychologically the viewpoint continued and was part of the atmosphere that his *Issei* parents had to confront, and even himself in his early years. When it came to minorities like the Japanese, their intent was not confrontation of injustice, simply how to cope with it. They expected injustice and discrimination one way or another.[48]

Thus, the Japanese American citizens accepted and resettled with remarkable grace and acquiescence. Cultural beliefs such as filial piety, father having the final word; *giri*, a social obligation to follow the strict rules and norms of society; *gaman*, enduring the seemingly unendurable quietly and with patience; *ninjo*, one's natural feeling of warmth and compassion for fellow humans; *otonashi*, the necessity of keeping one's place, remaining quiet, avoiding the appearance of knowing too much or voicing too many opinions were the foundation that enabled the Japanese to endure harsh injustice and profound humiliation, yet hold their heads high. These beliefs and resulting resilience also contribute to the "model minority" myth many cultures struggle with today.

Redemption and Reparations. The Immigration and Nationality Act of 1952 (the McCarran-Walter Act), despite maintaining racial discrimination, allowed Japanese immigrants to apply for citizenship. *Nisei* children coached their *Issei* parents on civics and American history for their exams.[49]

Many of the best and brightest among the 442nd veterans returned determined to challenge the power structure of Hawaii. Daniel Inouye, Spark Matsunaga, John Ushijima, and Katsugo "Kats" Miho took advantage of the GI Bill and entered law schools on the East Coast. Twenty-five other Hawaiian *Nisei* veterans studied law at George Washington or nearby Georgetown. They began to occupy positions of power in business, government, and the legal profession, altogether altering Hawaiian culture and society.

Under mounting pressure by Gordon Hirabayashi, Fred Korematsu, Minoru Yasui, the JACL, and other redress organizations, President Jimmy Carter opened an investigation in 1980 to determine whether the government decision to put Japanese Americans into concentration camps had been justified. He appointed the Commission on Wartime Relocation and Internment of Civilians to investigate the camps. Its report, *Personal Justice Denied,* was issued in December 1982 and concluded that President Roosevelt's issuance of Executive Order 9066 "was not justified by military necessity, and the decisions which followed from it . . . were not driven by analysis of military conditions. The broad historical causes which shaped these decisions were race prejudice, war hysteria, and a failure of political leadership. . . . A grave injustice was done to American citizens and resident aliens of Japanese ancestry who, without individual review or any probative evidence against them, were excluded, removed and detained by the United States during World War II." In its report to Congress, the Commission recommended a national apology and financial compensation to its surviving victims.[50]

In response to the Commission's report, Congress adopted the Civil Rights Act of 1988 to "acknowledge the fundamental injustice of the evacuation, relocation, and internment of United States citizens and permanent resident aliens of Japanese ancestry during World War II" and to "apologize on behalf of the people of the United States" for the internment of this racial minority. Congress confirmed in this Act that "these actions were carried out without adequate security reasons and without any acts of espionage or sabotage documented by the Commission and were motivated largely by racial prejudice, wartime hysteria, and a failure of political leadership. The excluded individuals of Japanese ancestry suffered enormous damages, both material and intangible, and there were incalculable losses in education and job training, all of which resulted in significant suffering for which appropriate compensation has not been made. For these fundamental violations of the basic civil liberties and constitutional rights of these individuals of Japanese ancestry, the Congress apologizes on behalf of the Nation."[51]

In 1987 activist members of the 442nd visited Congress, strategized with Japanese Americans such as Representatives Norman Mineta, Robert Matsui, Senators Spark Matsunaga and Daniel Inouye, to facilitate the Civil Liberties Act authorizing reparations to Japanese-Americans. They prevailed. When asked in an interview what legacy he felt that he and the 442nd had left for subsequent generations, Rudy Tokiwa responded, "I think my job has been done. I feel that, now, I don't have to do anything more. I think we — *not I but we* — have proven ourselves."[52]

On August 10, 1988, President Ronald Reagan told the American people that "we gather here today to right a grave wrong. More than 40 years ago, shortly after the bombing of

Pearl Harbor, 120,000 persons of Japanese ancestry living in the United States were forcibly removed from their homes and placed in makeshift internment camps. This action was taken without trial, without jury. It was based solely on race. ... For here we admit a wrong; here we reaffirm our commitment as a nation to equal justice under the law."

The Civil Liberties Act of 1988 signed by President Reagan also provided for payments of $20,000 to each of the remaining 60,000 survivors of the internment camps, although the President admitted that "no payment can make up for those lost years." [53]

On May 20, 2011 Acting Solicitor General of the United States Neal Katyal wrote the following: "By the time the cases of Gordon Hirabayashi and Fred Korematsu reached the Supreme Court, the Solicitor General [Charles Fahy] had learned of a key intelligence report that undermined the rationale behind the internment. *The Ringle Report*, from the Office of Naval Intelligence, found that only a small percentage of Japanese Americans posed a potential security threat, and that the most dangerous were already known or in custody. But the Solicitor General did not inform the Court of the report, despite warnings from Department of Justice attorneys that failing to alert the Court 'might approximate the suppression of evidence.' Instead, he argued that it was impossible to segregate loyal Japanese Americans from disloyal ones. Nor did he inform the Court that a key set of allegations used to justify the internment, that Japanese Americans were using radio transmitters to communicate with enemy submarines off the West Coast, had been discredited by the FBI and FCC. And to make matters worse, he relied on gross generalizations about Japanese Americans, such as that they were disloyal and motivated by 'racial solidarity.'"

"The Supreme Court upheld Hirabayashi's and Korematsu's convictions. And it took nearly a half century for courts to overturn these decisions. One court decision in the 1980s that did so highlighted the role played by the Solicitor General, emphasizing that the Supreme Court gave 'special credence' to the Solicitor General's representations. The court thought it unlikely that the Supreme Court would have ruled the same way had the Solicitor General exhibited complete candor. Yet those decisions still stand today as a reminder of the mistakes of that era."[54]

In his speech that followed on May 24, Katyal said "The mistakes the Justice Department made in defending Japanese internment during World War II did more than harm the reputation of the government. Ultimately it harmed our commitment to those magnificent words carved on the front of the Supreme Court, at the top: Equal Justice Under Law.

"Katyal examined what one DOJ lawyer called the suppression of evidence from the high court. At the time, Solicitor General Charles Fahy did not disclose a report from the Office of Naval Intelligence that undermined the legal rationale behind internment.

"Katyal quoted from Justice Stephen Breyer's book *Making Our Democracy Work: A Judge's View.* The *Korematsu* case, Breyer wrote, 'suggested that the Court was unable or unwilling to make an unpopular decision that would protect an unpopular minority.' Breyer said *Korematsu* 'harmed' the high court.

"I think it did harm the court," Katyal said. "But it obviously harmed others as well. It harmed approximately 120,000 Japanese Americans."[55]

In February 2020 The California Assembly apologized for discriminating against Japanese Americans and helping the

U.S. government deliver them to internment camps during World War II. The resolution passed unanimously the day after the Governor declared February 19 a Day of Remembrance, the date in 1942 when President Franklin D. Roosevelt signed Executive Order 9066.

After the votes, lawmakers gathered at the entrance of the chamber to hug and shake hands with victims and their families, former internees including 96-year-old Kiyo Sato, who said young people need to know about the 120,000 Japanese Americans who were sent to internment camps. "We need to remind them that this can't happen again."

The California resolution said anti-Japanese sentiment began in California as early as 1913, when the state passed the Alien Land Law targeting Japanese farmers who were perceived as a threat by some in the massive agricultural industry. Seven years later, the state barred anyone with Japanese ancestry from buying farmland.

"During the years leading up to World War II, California led the nation in fanning the flames of racism," said Assemblyman Al Muratsuchi. Senator Richard Pan, sponsor for the resolution in the state Senate, introduced two sons of former California U.S. Representative Norman Yoshio Mineta, who served in a presidential cabinet under Bill Clinton and next under George W. Bush. Mineta was imprisoned in a camp but went on to become "one of the most influential Asian Americans in the history of our nation," leading the congressional effort for the U.S. apology and reparations. Of note: California has the largest population of people of Japanese descent of any state, numbering roughly 430,000.[56]

PART THREE

From Exclusion to Inclusion

CHAPTER 5

Personal, Cultural, Institutional, and Systemic Exclusion

The concept of exclusion is the legal non-existence of individuals or groups by their continual absence from being part of the criteria to participate. Generations of Americans who have inherited racial bias towards people of color will continue to pass that bias on to their children and all future generations.

According to the United Nations' *Identifying Social Inclusion and Exclusion,* "Exclusion is a multidimensional phenomenon not limited to material deprivation, a state in which individuals are unable to participate fully in economic, social, political and cultural life. Exclusion is both an outcome and a process. Participation is hindered when people lack access to material resources including income, employment, land and housing, and to services such as education and health care. Participation is also limited when people cannot exercise their voice, and when their rights and dignity are not accorded equal respect and protection. Exclusion entails not only material deprivation but also lack of agency or control over important decisions as well as feelings of alienation and inferiority. In nearly all countries, to varying degrees, age, sex, disability, race, ethnicity, religion, migration status, socioeconomic status, place of residence, sexual orientation and gender identity have been grounds for social exclusion.

"Inclusion is the process of improving the terms of participation in society, particularly for people who are disadvantaged, through enhanced opportunities, access to resources, voice and respect for rights. Inclusion is both a process and a goal. The issues are multidimensional, relational, and dynamic along a continuum between the two states."[1]

Not all exclusions are racially based. Those are simply often the most visible, based on ethnicity and color of skin. In almost every culture or nation of origin, there is a bias of "colorism," light skin being preferable to dark. When applied to individuals or groups, there is an interconnection among characterizations such as race, gender, class, or caste, which creates overlapping layers and interdependent systems of discrimination and disadvantage.

Exclusion has myriad faces, resulting in a wide variety of dehumanizing consequences. Exclusions range from individual preferences to culturally learned biases, ultimately to systemic exclusion, which perpetuates discrimination and promotes the belief that certain groups are superior, others of lesser value.

Systemic exclusion impacts individuals and groups in every stage of life through the institutional exclusions (legal and extralegal) in education, banking and finance, housing, criminal justice, and public health. They can range from casual cruelties known as microaggressions to accumulations that may result in violence.

Personal or Internalized Exclusion is an individual classification of race-based beliefs and feelings, ranging from preferences regarding diet, social and cultural activities, religious, philosophical, and political beliefs to biases toward individuals, racial and ethnic groups. These biases often reflect the acceptance of parental views, perceptions, and prejudices, sometimes excluding factual information contradicting these views. These personal preferences can be conscious or unconscious, positive or negative, associations. These biases are the basis of the ideology of racism and white superiority.

Cultural or Interpersonal Exclusion is an inherited acceptance of bigotry and biases shown between individuals through word and action, a reflection of one's cultural group, preferences, and decisions. These distinctions include ethnic history, religion, traditions, holidays, celebrations, dietary restrictions, even perpetuation of negative social constructs. For example, misunderstood stereotypes of Native Americans and their tribal traditions are depicted as wild, uncivilized, uncultured, foreign, and unacceptable, to be shunned.[2] Ironically, the tribes have a stronger sense of humanitarianism, and a spiritual relationship with the animal kingdom and nature, in contrast to the capitalistic concerns of American immigrants, including the Founders. Biases toward stereotypes can be projected onto every ethnic minority in America today.

Cultural diversity is a training methodology, constructed as an individual-change process, teaching universally acceptable elements found in all ethnic cultural groups; educational and informative, it does not require the development of individual skills nor change. The educational model of cultural diversity introduces and displays unique cultures and traditions, language, religious beliefs, ethnic foods, music, dance, and celebratory events.

Never before has our cultural diversity threatened our survival as a democratic nation. "The world is watching America, the only great power in history made up of people from every corner of the planet, comprising every race and faith and cultural practice, to see if our experiment in democracy can work. To see if we can actually live up to the meaning of our creed."[3]

Institutional Exclusion refers to the existence of systematic policies or laws and practices that provide differential access to society's goods, services, and opportunities by race. This results in unfair policies and discriminatory practices within organizations and institutions such as schools and workplaces that routinely produce racially inequitable outcomes for people of color and advantages for white people. Individuals within institutions take on the institution's power when they reinforce racial inequities through discriminatory policies and practices within the institutions.

Systemic Exclusion is racial bias among institutions and across society involving the cumulative and compounding effects of an array of factors, including the history, culture, ideology and interactions of institutions and policies that systematically privilege white people and disadvantage people of color.

This is the most complex and enduring form of exclusion. Spanning generations, it becomes an unchallenged way of life. Systemic exclusion affects every ethnic and cultural group, albeit to different degrees and intensities. America's form of systemic exclusion targets all people with distinct differences from the majority white group.

* * * * *

Discrimination is a group phenomenon consisting of three overlapping layers of exclusion addressing specific group characteristics. Both secondary and tertiary categories are impacted by the primary category of color or ethnicity.

Primary Exclusion is a historical omission of specific groups by ethnicity or color or gender. The most salient example is slavery, which resulted in the omission of African Americans in creating the U.S. Constitution. Another example is legislation such as the Chinese Exclusion Act of 1882, terminating immigration of Chinese laborers who were competing with white citizens and European immigrants for employment. Ethnicity and color are primary factors for the foundation of systemic exclusion in America.

The victims of systemic exclusion are powerless to stop bias and discriminatory beliefs without the recognition and support of the beneficiaries of exclusion: the white majority. Without change among the white majority, the concept of lesser value for the excluded groups is passed on from generation to generation. This cycle is the power and longevity of unchallenged systemic exclusion which can be broken only when the majority white group concedes that they, too, will benefit from systemic change. The cycle may break naturally resulting from our impending population demographics shift, when whites are no longer the majority group.

Secondary Exclusions are fundamentally invisible, and functionally *"persona non grata,"* Latin for "unwelcome person." This category wields its power and impact across all ethnic and cultural groups in America. Because Anglo Christian males created our systems and institutions, all "other" groups such as women, gays, the physically-challenged, and different religious populations clamored for recognition and inclusion.

For example, physically challenged and disabled individuals in America were legally non-existent until the Americans with Disabilities Act (ADA) was signed into law in July 1990, by President George H.W. Bush.[4]

Before the groundbreaking law, this group of disabled individuals, including the mentally impaired, were invisible to most members of the group of non-disabled individuals, resulting in buildings and structures being designed and constructed without the consideration of disabled individuals' needs as potential participants in the projects.

The ADA mandated engineers and architects to retroactively make modifications such as ramps, expanded entrances to buildings, restrooms, elevators, and dedicated parking spaces. It is important to note that because this category affects white individuals *and* people of color, our government acted swiftly, taking the important step of creating a systemic solution, implementing the formula of inclusion by expanding the criteria for participation. The fact that the majority-white group benefited, in addition to people of color, was the pivotal impetus for systemic change. The factor of disability is now included in the design and building of all new structures, and the continuous retrofitting of previously constructed non-compliant buildings.

This has resulted in the concept of Universal Design, which has become one of the foundations for equitable reform of institutions as a means of eliminating barriers, from both a physical and metaphorical perspective.

Tertiary Exclusions affect less visible than ethnically distinct or physically impaired groups because their differences are not readily identifiable. These groups can be as diverse as religious intolerances or as unremarkable and seemingly benign as left-handedness. The classification adversely affects individuals of the majority group.

The Lesbian, Gay, Bi-Sexual, Transgender, and Queer or Questioning (LGBTQ) group did not exist for protection under the law until June 2020, when the Supreme Court ruled their legitimate existence citing the Civil Rights Act prohibition of employment discrimination based on sexual orientation or gender identity.

The recognition opened the door for LGBTQ groups to demand an Equality Act be passed into law by Congress, to provide consistent and explicit non-discrimination protections for LGBTQ people across essential areas of life including employment, housing credit, education, public spaces and services, federally funded services, and jury service. The Equality Act was passed by the House of Representatives by a bipartisan vote in March 2020.[5]

The issue of discrimination towards LGBTQ became more public when the Clinton Administration passed the official military policy of "Don't ask, don't tell" (DADT) in December 1993, which exemplified the need for these groups to remain invisible, and not to demand their opportunity to participate. Openly gay individuals were not allowed to serve in the military until 2011, when President Obama officially ended the DADT policy.[6] President Biden signed an Executive Order to remove the ban of transgender individuals from serving in the military in January 2021.[7]

Left-handed children were once converted to right-handed, in accord with cursive writing and computational exercises, which we have since learned created a speech deficiency in these children known as stuttering.[8] Since we no longer forcibly convert the left-handed to become right-handed, there has been a dramatic reduction in speech deficiencies. Other examples are scissors designed for right-handed children; and desks with a pop-up writing table, similar to airline food trays, rising on the right side.

These discrepancies are not necessarily malicious in intent, but a natural product of exclusion of non-mainstream individuals, exemplifying the predictable result of omission of those individuals from the criteria for participation.

CHAPTER 6

Race, Ethnicity, and Cultural Identity

Race is a social construct that describes people with shared physical characteristics. It can have tremendous social significance in terms of opportunities, status, wealth and behavioral health services, according to U.S. Department of Health and Human Services (HHS), *Improving Cultural Competence.*[1]

Race. Although often thought to be based on genetic traits (e.g., skin color), there is no reliable means of identifying race based on genetic information. What we perceive as diverse races (based largely on selective physical characteristics, such as skin color) are much more genetically similar than different. Moreover, physical characteristics ascribed to a particular racial group can also appear in those not in that group. Asians, for example, often have an epicanthic eye fold, but this characteristic is also shared by the Kung San bushmen, an African nomadic Tribe.[2]

Ethnicity. Ethnicity differs from race in that groups of people can share a common racial ancestry yet have very different ethnic identities. Thus, by definition, ethnicity, unlike race, is an explicitly cultural phenomenon. It is based on a shared cultural or family heritage and shared values and beliefs rather than shared physical characteristics.

Although sometimes used interchangeably with "race," it is important to draw distinctions between the two. Ethnicity refers to the social identity and mutual sense of belonging that defines a group of people through common historical or family origins, beliefs, and standards of behavior (i.e., culture). In some cases, ethnicity also refers to identification with a clan or group whose identity can be based on race and culture. Some Latinx, for example, self-identify in terms of both their ethnicity (e.g., their Cuban heritage) and their race (e.g., whether they are dark or light skinned).[3]

Cultural Identity. Cultural identity describes an individual's affiliation or identification with a particular group or groups. Cultural identities are not static; they develop and change across stages of the life cycle. People reevaluate their cultural identities and sometimes resist, rebel, or reformulate them over time. Within a community, race, or nation, people belong to multiple cultural groups, each with their own cultural norms. All people, regardless of race or ethnicity, develop a cultural identity. Individuals can hold two or more cultural identities simultaneously.

Language is a primary element of culture. Styles of communication and nonverbal methods of communication are also important aspects of cultural groups. Issues such as the use of direct versus indirect communication, appropriate personal space, social parameters for and displays of physical contact, use of silence, preferred ways of moving, meaning of gestures, the degree to which arguments and verbal confrontations are acceptable, the degree of formality expected in communication, and amount of eye contact expected, are all culturally defined and reflect very basic ethnic and cultural differences.

For example, most Asian Americans come from high-context cultural groups in which sensitive messages are encoded carefully to avoid giving offense. African Americans have a relatively high-context culture compared with Anglo

Americans but a somewhat lower-context culture compared with Asian Americans. Thus, African Americans typically rely to a greater degree than Anglo Americans on nonverbal cues in communicating. Conversely, Anglo American culture is low context (as are some European cultural groups, such as German and British); communication is expected to be explicit, and formal information is conveyed primarily through the literal content of spoken or written messages.[4]

Acculturation is the process whereby an individual from one cultural group learns and adopts elements of another cultural group, integrating them into their original culture. This is typically used to describe how an immigrant or non-majority individual or group adopts cultural elements from the majority or mainstream culture.

Assimilation is one outcome of acculturation. It involves the complete adoption of the ways of life of the new cultural group, resulting in the assimilated group losing nearly all of its original or native culture. America's stringent assimilation process has resulted in eliminating ethnic roots, cultural affiliation, and diverse languages within three generations. Every generation becomes more distant from its nation of origin.

Biculturalism occurs when an individual acquires the knowledge, skills, and identity of both their culture of origin and the mainstream/majority culture, and is equally capable of social and cultural interaction in both societies.

Enculturation is a process whereby an individual begins to learn about and comes to value the native culture that surrounds him or her (similar to acculturation), and adopts that culture.[5]

Internalized racism comprises personal beliefs and biases about race and racism as influenced by our culture, including prejudice towards others of a different race and internalized oppression (the negative beliefs about oneself by people of color, or internalized privilege) or beliefs about superiority or entitlement by white people.[6] It is a learned belief, not a genetic one. The recipient of racism is based on physical traits, but the perpetuation of racism is learned and transferred. The multi-generational transference of racism is the root of systemic racism and a direct byproduct of the institution of slavery.

Systemic racism is the product and manifestation of generations of individual and institutional racism. It is exclusion, inequitable opportunity for participation, and without options for a solution. The extremes of individual racism are superiority and hate, including the zero-sum mentality that any benefits accrued by people of color result in an equal loss of white majority benefits. These attitudes, perpetuated through generations of misinformation and family biases, have created an almost insurmountable intergenerational oppression of our Black communities.

Sociologists raise the question of whether prejudice is a hereditary product or a learned product. Prejudice is learned, but how and where is it learned? More importantly, how is it taught? Prejudice is an opinion, prejudgment, or attitude about a group or its members. Prejudice can be positive, but is more often a bias of negativity. Prejudices are often accompanied by ignorance, fear, or in the extreme, hatred.

Social scientists believe children begin to acquire prejudices and stereotypes as toddlers. Many studies have shown that children are exposed to prejudice as early as age three. Children pick up terms of racial prejudice without really understanding their significance. Their family becomes the core of their group, and they develop positive or negative attitudes about other racial or ethnic groups, or "out-groups." Once learned, prejudice and bias resist change, even when evidence fails to support them or points to the contrary. More serious is the existence of hidden bias, mental residue from years of overt and covert exposure to discriminatory acts and behaviors.

The issue of hidden bias is exemplified in the current explosion of police killings of Black men and women in American cities. In these cases, police bias may affect their split-second life-or-death decisions to fire their weapons. Police officers incorrectly assumed Black individuals were holding guns, a hidden bias, and instantly acted upon those learned instincts with immediate and fatal consequences.

"Project Implicit" is an international collaboration of researchers maintained by Harvard University, the University of Washington, and the University of Virginia, administering hundreds of thousands of online implicit association tests designed to detect hidden racial biases. The tests find not only that three-quarters of whites have an implicit pro-white, anti-Black bias, but also that nearly as many Latinx and Asians share that pro-white, anti-Black bias.[7] Systemic racism is pervasive and impacts everyone, including people of color.

"The Hidden Prejudice Program at Harvard" established a scientific way to identify unconscious bias that can lead to discriminatory behavior and in turn, racial inequality. The Implicit Association Test determines, utilizing a binary scale of measurement, the degree of hidden bias in individuals.[8]

Can science be significant in reducing and eventually eradicating so many years of fear, hatred, discrimination, and unnecessary pain caused by overt and hidden biases?

According to Carl Sagan, "Science is much more of a way of thinking than it is a body of knowledge." [9] If quantification and logic were factors to mitigate racism, then it would suggest that outlawing racism could be a reasonable solution. Science and logic cannot alter the generational development of hatred and discriminatory beliefs and attitudes. Science can be a resource and justification for the altering of hateful beliefs and attitudes, but the action extends beyond the reach of science and is decidedly human.

The process of inclusion is the path to the eradication of racism. Because exclusion is a group phenomenon, and racism is a bias toward a group, when inclusion is successfully implemented, everyone will be viewed and judged as an individual, thus eliminating group bias, and ultimately racism. In other words, *see the individual,* hold the individual accountable. *Do not assume the individual represents the group.*

Identity and Identification

An essential aspect of human emotional development is the formation of self-concept, or identity, a sense of who one is, and a consciousness of one's relationship with other people. Children's growing self-awareness shifts from concrete physical attributes to more abstract characteristics. Young children, four to six years of age, define themselves in observable characteristics such as hair color, height, or favorite activities.[10]

Within a few years, descriptions of themselves shift to more abstract, internal, or psychological qualities, including their competencies and skills relative to others. Adolescents increasingly define themselves by the unique and individual quality of their feelings, thoughts, and beliefs rather than simply by external characteristics.

The ethnic, cultural, and religious groups in which a child is reared are significant components of a child's self-concept. A child who is a member of a distinctive or specific group has usually created a mental category for that group by ages five to six years. Children from ethnic minorities tend to be more aware of ethnic differences than are non-minority children.[11]

Children tend to identify with those persons to whom they are emotionally attached and whom they perceive to be similar to themselves in some way, incorporating the characteristics of parents and other influential persons by adopting their appearance, attitudes, and behavior. Role models children emulate may have negative and positive characteristics, thus influencing children in undesirable and beneficial ways.[12] An influential venue for critical social concepts is visual media. The most successful children's program *Sesame Street* debuted in 1969 on what is now the Public Broadcasting Service (PBS). *Sesame Street* made a conscious decision to be a multicultural program emphasizing inclusion by the diversity of their Muppet characters. Jim Henson's characters were Asian, Hispanic, Indigenous, African American, white, physically-challenged or disabled, autistic, AIDS-infected, and straddling-the-lines-of-sexual-orientation Muppets.

Their 50th Anniversary Show celebrated accessibility in over 60 countries worldwide, translated to an excess of 70 languages. They were awarded a $100 million MacArthur grant to provide educational programs for refugee children and children in Africa's AIDS-devastated country.[13]

Academic versus Empirical Learning

First-person and Third-person Learning. Does third-person comprehension of information and history equal first-person experience in bridging the chasm of bias and discrimination? In admitting white privilege, can one appreciate the depths of pain caused by systemic racism? As long as exclusion and systemic racism exist, all experiences of excluded groups are linked to their recognizably distinct physical characteristics.

There are schools in California and New York attempting to bridge the third-person medium of learning to the first-person experience by requiring high school students to participate in community-based activities for school credit, ideally adding significant experience to their college application resume. If required for college acceptance, cultural diversity can become a legitimate factor in establishing which students are more qualified for college entrance.

The march toward equality has been chronicled from slavery to emancipation, from segregation to desegregation, in civil rights marches, legislative actions, academic modifications, race riots, and Black Lives Matter protests, nationwide and international.

There is a vast proliferation of literature sharing vivid and life-altering revelations of what it is like to be Black in America, Black in other countries, and the uniquely American history of slavery. Educating oneself can be a pivotal step in helping to create a solution to inequality.

Participative learning is integral to individual comprehension of systemic racism and its impact on people of color. Academic education rarely reaches people emotionally, thus not enabling individuals to empathize and internalize the horror of racism.

I often heard the phrase, "whoever wins the war gets to write the history," but that does not mandate an unquestioning and absolute acceptance of and obedience to institutionalized information. "It is very natural that the history written by the victim" said a Mexican in 1874, "does not altogether chime with the story of the victor." [14]

* * * *

Maya Angelou understood how a laugh could be a survival mechanism. In 1988 she described to a predominantly white audience in Salado, Texas, how a maid's smile inspired *"The Mask,"* written to honor the woman riding a bus in New York City, carrying two shopping bags, who laughed whenever the bus stopped abruptly. She also laughed when it stopped slowly. Angelou said "I thought, hmmm, uh huh . . . Now, if you don't know Black features, you may think she's laughing, but she wasn't laughing. She was simply extending her lips and making a sound — ha, ha, ha, ha." "Oh, I see. That's that survival apparatus."

> Seventy years in these folks' world
> The child I works for calls me 'girl'
> I say "Ha! Ha! Ha! Yes ma'am!"
> For workin's sake
> I'm too proud to bend and
> Too poor to break
> So — ha, ha, ha, ha — I laugh! Until my
>   stomach ache
> When I think about myself.[15]

Our Jewish immigrants have suffered unfathomable horrors, yet have mastered the art of self-deprecation in their unique and sardonic humor. Entertainment created for its own audiences in small clubs in New York City, expanding to Jewish-dominated resorts in the Catskills known as the Borscht Belt, as well as in Pennsylvania's Pocono Mountains,[16] Jewish humor contributed a remarkable number of America's comedic geniuses: Woody Allen, Mel Brooks, Lenny Bruce, Billy Crystal, Julia Louis-Dreyfus, Groucho Marx, Gilda Radner, Joan Rivers, Amy Schumer, Sarah Silverman, Jon Stewart, Jerry Seinfeld, to name a few.

The point of this observation is that we can develop new methods, platforms, and venues to inform, educate, and change the way each of us comprehends both systemic racism and anti-Semitic behaviors. Once communication channels are established, it becomes easier to educate and to alter bias and discrimination towards excluded groups.

Activist Eldridge Cleaver wrote, "There is no more neutrality in the world. You either have to be part of the solution, or you're going to be part of the problem." [17] Individuals of the majority white population have essentially two options as citizens. (1) As representatives of their group, white individuals who have concluded they must not disassociate from the atrocities executed by their group are committed to preventing repetition of those deeds. They accept guilt by association, group identification, and the responsibility to correct the problems associated with the sin of slavery, including reparations. (2) White individuals who do not associate with the actions of their group or its history ("I do not own slaves and none of my family owned slaves") reject group identification, association, and responsibility for actions committed by whites in the past. They epitomize the benefits of inclusion: to be seen and judged as an individual, without direct association with, nor responsibility for, their racial group and its history.

Inclusion is a luxury that excluded groups such as Blacks, Native Americans, Latinx, Asian Americans, Pacific Islanders, and women do not enjoy. Without inclusion, they will forever be identified as minority individuals and excluded groups.

Social Justice Ally. Allies have a common interest with those they desire to help. In an alliance, both parties stand to benefit from the bond or connection they share. In the field of social justice studies, becoming an ally to another person or group has become a vital concept in examining issues of oppression and privilege.[19]

An ally is a person of one social identity group who stands up in support of members of a different group, typically a member of a dominant group standing beside members of a group being discriminated against or treated unjustly. Regardless of our identity, all of us benefit when we take steps toward eliminating prejudice and discrimination in our society. We benefit from our collective efforts to create a better-educated and more understanding world that treats each of us with dignity, respect, and equality. As Dr. Martin Luther King, Jr. said, "Injustice anywhere is a threat to justice everywhere." [20]

An ally is someone whose personal commitment to fighting oppression and prejudice is reflected in the willingness to (1) educate oneself about different identities and experiences, (2) challenge one's discomfort and prejudices, (3) learn and practice the skills of being an ally, and (4) take action to create interpersonal, societal and institutional change. The words often attributed to Gandhi reflect the spirit of being an ally, "Be the change you wish to see in the world." [21]

Allyship in the Workplace. Harvard Business Review suggests "allyship [is] a strategic mechanism used by individuals to become collaborators, accomplices, and coconspirators who fight injustice and promote equity in the workplace through supportive personal relationships and public acts of sponsorship and advocacy. Allies endeavor to drive systemic improvements to workplace policies, practices, and culture." [22]

CHAPTER 7

Individual, Institutional, and Systemic Inclusion

Individual Change. "A journey of a thousand miles begins with a single step," wrote Lao Tzu. The willingness to accept the need for individual change and to challenge the status quo perpetuated by the dominant culture are the monumental steps toward a solution to injustice, discrimination, and exclusion. It requires a commitment to new ideas, experiences, diverse opinions, and change. It is an awakening to fallacious information, the omissions and denial of actual American experiences, and the need to disrupt that reality. Individual change is the progenitor to institutional and systemic change.

Individual change for the benefit of others is the most crucial and difficult step toward systemic change. It is not an either/or equation, but a continuum process to eliminate barriers, and identify measurements of success. This continuum is derived from the exclusion of minority groups and does not address included majority group issues. The inclusion continuum for change is from exclusion to non-exclusion and from non-inclusion to inclusion.

> Exclusion → Non-Exclusion → Non-Inclusion → Inclusion

Exclusion is the absence of groups from the criteria for participation which renders an individual non-existent and invisible. Exclusion is a group phenomenon with the absence of individual participation.

Non-Exclusion is the recognition of group existence while still lacking inclusion in the existing criteria for individual participation.

Non-Inclusion is the recognition of individual existence, and the creation of additional options for participation, such as Ethnic Studies or Special Education. This accommodation does not require the original system design to change; instead it creates Separate but Equal satellite venues that do not offer full inclusion.

Inclusion is the process whereby institutions and systems expand its criteria for participation, such as integrating Ethnic Studies into U.S. History, promoting the development of multilingual educational programs, and mainstreaming Special Education students into the general curriculum.

This solution reciprocally benefits the physically challenged and non-physically challenged because non-physically challenged students will be introduced to, and better prepared for, all participants in the world of inclusion. The promotion of equity and inclusion benefits everyone, the excluded, marginally included whites, and fully included whites.

Cross-Cultural Literacy, Institutional and Systemic Diversity

New models for cooperation and collaboration with culturally diverse countries are needed to meet the demand created by domestic and global expansion. This challenge established the need for cross-cultural literacy capabilities to facilitate trading agreements with other countries.

The globalization of technology enabled countries all over the world to access information and resources to shape and rebuild infrastructures, become financially independent, and globally competitive. China, South Korea, Japan, and

India, are some of the beneficiaries of this evolution, known as the Asian Miracle,[1] and have risen to become competitive economies in the production of automobiles, televisions, computers, and agriculture.

America realized that its era of economic and cultural dominance had been drastically eroded and found itself needing to collaborate to establish new trade formulas. Without strategic planning, America outsourced production to less costly countries with cheaper labor and facilities, and undermined its traditional industries and American employment.

Multiple-language capability is the Achilles heel of American business. America's early dominance in economic and scientific fields coerced the rest of the world to make accommodations; for example, other countries had to become fluent in English because we refused to learn their languages and international scientists had to accept our unwillingness to adopt the metric system of measurement. We have begun to recognize our cross-cultural competency deficits and the necessary adaptations we must make to remain competitive in a global economy.

Teledyne Ryan Aeronautical. Early in my diversity consulting career, I worked with Teledyne Ryan Aeronautical in Southern California, with global clients for their technical products. One of their primary clients was Japan, who purchased several of their newly developed aeronautical products. The Japanese came to Teledyne Ryan to observe the technical components and learn how to operate them effectively before making the multi-million dollar investment. Satisfaction with both the technology and their ability to manage it enabled them to make the purchases. Several months after the purchase, the Japanese ran into some technical problems with the new equipment; naturally, they requested assistance from the creator, Teledyne Ryan.

Initially, Teledyne Ryan patiently provided the information through visual technical assistance, with constant verification from the Japanese that they comprehended the instructions. This process became very frustrating for both sides and Teledyne Ryan was losing their patience with the lack of a solution to this very costly problem. Their desire for continued sales to the Japanese tempered their frustrations. The principal issue was the technical explanations to the dysfunction and the corresponding assertions by the Japanese of comprehending the necessary adjustments.

I explained to the Senior Management of Teledyne Ryan that culturally, the Japanese will always affirm comprehension after detailed explanations because they are too embarrassed to say otherwise. Their cultural expectation is that one would realize the problem is never going to be solved with a distant telecommunications approach. I recommended they send the technical experts to Japan to demonstrate, using a participative learning model, the necessary modifications for resolving the technical impediments.

After the trip to Japan, the Japanese were not only satisfied but also grateful for the cultural accommodation, and they purchased even more equipment because they were confident of technical support when necessary. Developing cross-cultural literacy is not a complicated problem or barrier in resolving crucial issues with different countries and cultural groups. It is a critical and imperative business competency in an ever-expanding global economy.

Institutional Diversity in the Workplace

This product or outcome requires an institutional model for

change. It requires the understanding and belief that individuals from different ethnic and cultural backgrounds will visualize, interpret, and analyze with a unique perspective. The goal for all businesses and industries is to identify and select the best minds to cultivate, enhance, and expand their lines of work to their ultimate level of performance.

Ironically, a universal assumption is that every individual believes they are *already* performing at that level. The dilemma is that the business design and methodology do not select and develop the culturally-diverse capabilities of all employees in their work systems.

America is an individual-based performance model with rewards, salaries, and promotions provided to the most capable individuals. The individual is the main criterion for performance and measurement for both the self and the organization.

Systemic diversity encourages individuals from cultures that value sacrifice, dedication, and cooperation to a group performance model. Hence, the Japanese success model, introduced in 1962 by the Nippon Wireless and Telegraph Company, was a group model coined "Quality Circles." [2]

Individuals working in groups "to identify, analyze, and solve work-related problems" became the model to produce innovative designs in electronics, and later, in the automobile industry. America attempted to replicate the model, but it is impossible to expect an individual-based model for success to adapt itself into a group model. Systemic diversity challenges institutions to incorporate the process of inclusion in their transitions to new models for success.

Inclusion in the workplace is "the practice or policy of providing equal access to opportunities and resources for people who might otherwise be excluded or marginalized."

American employers must grasp that they cannot successfully implement diversity without the corresponding expansion of inclusion into its organizational culture.

Diversity encompasses the unique traits, values, customs, and characteristics that each individual brings to the work environment. Inclusion is achieved when an organization cultivates each individual to their maximum capability, and that diversity becomes the organization's culture.

Systemic inclusion begins with recognition of the absence of diversity and the acceptance that it is detrimental to the success of an organization. The process of inclusion has its greatest opportunity for implementation when promoted as a goal to ensure the success and survival of the organization.

Stages on the inclusion continuum are illustrated by the advertising and marketing industries. The most vital factor in America is economic. We now see diversity in almost all advertisements of products and services, representing the stage of non-exclusion rather than inclusion.

You will not see a McDonald's commercial without African American servers or clients as central participants demonstrating the franchise's nod to non-exclusion. Their presence is an acknowledgment that they exist, fundamental to eradicating exclusion and a major step towards the ultimate goal of inclusion. However, the process of pursuing inclusion is far more complex and time-consuming than changing the characters in media and ads. McDonald's has altered its marketing ads in recognition that Blacks are a significant portion of its fast food industry market share. It is merely a business decision rather than a moral or equity commitment to institutional inclusion.

Research has demonstrated that women have a more cooperative and participative model for managing personnel than the male-dominated top-down style, representing alternative models for leadership, innovation development, and change.[3] High-tech companies such as Apple, Microsoft, Google, Facebook, and Twitter have deployed unique models of leadership and employee participation in an attempt to thrive in a competitive global marketplace. They have a long way to go to counter the prevalence of white male styles of leadership.

A segment of our population continues to deny the need for institutional change because they are beneficiaries of the current exclusion system. Inclusion must be perceived as a win-win option for everyone to have any chance of success.

Institutional Inclusion

Inclusion is a process requiring diverse individuals and groups to formulate new policies and procedures, enabling our institutions and systems to move forward with equity. The participative process is indispensable to modifying institutional and organizational culture bias.

For example, physically challenged individuals have not had equitable access to employment. They were not included in the development teams of engineers and architects to design building structures. The teams predictably designed based upon the assumption that the participants would be like themselves.

Over time, the employees who came to work in these facilities expanded to include physically challenged individuals. Because they had been excluded from the design process, they were literally unable to enter buildings. Accommodations were developed to correct design flaws, resulting in the creation of ramps, larger doors, elevators for multi-floored buildings, and special parking accommodations. This cycle is a prime example of a Design of Omission.

The short-term solution is to include the physically challenged in the development of all future public and private facilities. The long term solution is to ensure that physically challenged individuals and all other excluded groups are facilitated by educational opportunities enabling them to become whatever their talents and aspiration dictate; hopefully, some will become structural engineers and architects.

Inclusion is the process to expand the criteria for participation of all individuals and groups. Inclusion is only possible when the excluded participate in the creation of policies and procedures for the success of an organization or institution.

Center for Independent Living. Supported by the California Department of Rehabilitation, students and community members collaborated to form The Center for Independent Living, Inc. (CIL) in 1972.[4]

Dedication, perseverance, and foresight created an alternate reality for severely disabled individuals. This new lifestyle exemplified the vision of the Physically Disabled Students Program (PDSP),[6] which was a radical departure from past practices in the medical and rehabilitation fields. (1) Those who know best the needs of disabled people and how to meet those needs are the disabled people themselves. (2) The needs of the disabled can be met most effectively by comprehensive programs which provide a variety of services. (3) Disabled people must be integrated into their community. The groundwork laid by the PDSP was invaluable in defining the general approach and methodology the Center for Independent Living would follow.

As the population of disabled citizens in Berkeley grew during the early 1980s, it became clear that the public bus system was not adequately providing for the daily needs of the disabled.

The Center for Independent Living requested that the Berkeley City Council address the public transportation needs of its disabled citizens. They provided the City Council with specific data of the seven bus lines that were the most necessary and beneficial for the disabled, but did not provide handicap accessibility. After considerable discussion, the City Council proposed establishing a handicap-accessible van system along those routes, to operate on Monday-Wednesday-Friday at specifically designated times. When this was rejected as an inadequate solution, the Council agreed to run them every day at specifically designated times, believing this to be a generous solution to the problem.

Separate but Equal remedies are never equal, merely accommodations rather than solutions, quick fixes without changing the system or inconveniencing the majority population. Whether the problem was institutional or systemic led to many spirited and heated discussions regarding accessibility, and the more significant issues of equity and access to public transportation.

After prolonged meetings, the CIL requested the budget for the public bus system which provided the replacement of older buses every 1–3 years. Since there was an average of ten new buses purchased every 1–3 years, the CIL requested keeping the van system in place while purchasing only new buses equipped with handicap accessibility. They also recommended the new buses be introduced on those routes most used by the handicapped.

The City of Berkeley started with a public bus system that excluded the disabled from participation. With the inclusion of the excluded group, the disabled, they expanded the criteria for participation and created a solution: handicap accessible buses. The City of Berkeley soon learned that the newly equipped handicap accessible buses also benefited the elderly, parents with strollers, and students with bicycles. Systemic change resulting from inclusion often benefits more than the originally targeted excluded group.

Bell Communications Research of New Jersey. Systemic diversity models do not always require drastic reconstruction of existing business systems. Often problems can be remedied with modifications to policies and procedures.

While working with Bell Communications Research of New Jersey, a problem surfaced when a newly-formed department began experiencing technical issues with its new computer systems. In analyzing the circumstances, a diversity issue was recognized. Some of the latest technical engineer hires were Chinese, whose primary language was Mandarin. To expedite resolution of problems, engineers began communicating with each other in Mandarin, despite the company policy requiring that only English be spoken on the job. This systemic diversity issue created a legitimate business problem that required a creative solution, yet the established procedures restricted its resolution.

Since the engineers responsible for solving this problem were all first-generation Chinese, the use of Mandarin was the most expedient way to communicate. When informed that the use of Mandarin was solely for business purposes, management recognized it was an acceptable exception to the standard policy of English as the only spoken language. Institutional change enables organizations to realize the benefits of modifying and expanding their criteria for participation.

Major League Baseball. In the early 1900s, Major League Baseball (MLB) focused on the popularity of its white players. The personal success in the majority group is not always a measurement of equity and equal opportunity. It is more often an example of the lack of proportional participation of minority groups in American institutions. The superiority of talent in MLB had always been suspect because of the exclusion of African American baseball players, who were forced to establish their own [Separate but Equal] Negro League Baseball.

In December 2020, Major League Baseball took a monumental step towards inclusion by no longer excluding the Negro Leagues. "Addressing what MLB described as a 'long overdue recognition', [the] Commissioner ... bestowed Major League status upon seven professional Negro Leagues that operated between 1920 and 1948. The decision means that the approximately 3,400 players of the Negro Leagues during this time period are officially considered Major Leagues, with their stats and records becoming a part of Major League history."[5] This is a huge achievement and represents one institution's willingness to eliminate the Separate but Equal status of non-white participants and to expand their original participation criteria to include these previously excluded participants. This is an historic event that legitimizes inclusion for the future of America, a benchmark and stellar example of systemic change for equality.

CHAPTER 8

Systemic Exclusions to Equal Opportunity

Women and Sexism

Women across the globe fit into the primary exclusion category, but in America, it becomes complicated due to white supremacy. White women in the United States have a unique classification due to racism. White men are influenced by the sexism that affects their spouses and daughters. The 19th Amendment to the Constitution gave women the right to vote, yet only "white women." Women of color were excluded from the benefits of the Amendment. Notably, color is always the most significant factor among primary, secondary, and tertiary exclusion parameters.

All aspects of identity enrich women's experiences, compounding and complicating the various oppressions and marginalizations they face. It becomes impossible to distinguish many of the injustices because women experience them intersectionally. Established systems such as the workplace can also be based solely on sex (pay, leave, healthcare benefits, etc.); it is engrained in institutions and contracts before women are even hired.

During the United Nations Fourth World Conference on Women held in Beijing 1995, Hillary Clinton addressed the global participants with the iconic statement, *"women's rights are human rights,"* [1] which is inherently accurate, but interpreted vastly differently in countries other than America. The impact on women outside of the United States ranges from denial of birth control to voting, access to education, driving an automobile, presence in public without a male escort, misogynist sexual and physical abuse, even lawful homicide. Australia, one of the most supportive nations on women's rights, has created a cabinet-level Office for Women.

In the United States, President Biden was one of the rare individuals with political power to recognize women's rights as essential to a democratic republic. He established a Gender Policy Council with the staff, leadership, and authority to ensure that agencies governing national security, healthcare, and economics consider the impact of their policies on the lives of women in particular.[2]

One of the American institutions experiencing the most tremendous challenge integrating women as equal participants is the U.S. military. The history of sexual harassment and sexual abuse in the military has been ignored and treated as a non-existent issue. Recent deaths of women by military personnel have elevated the issue to national spotlight, citing egregious neglect and lack of leadership in addressing the increasing occurrences.

Previously all-male institutions such as police and fire departments are adjusting their cultures toward change and the inclusion of women. Complicating this problem in America is the color issue, which permeates all systems and institutions, causing women of color to address the color issue before the gender issue. Because it affects white women, like the 19th Amendment, the issue of gender bias will always be a consideration for movements of change.

The Tomb of the Unknown Soldier, famed memorial in Arlington National Cemetery, had its first all-female guard change in history during September 2021. "It wasn't anyone's intent to 'engineer' this event, but we knew an event like this had significant meaning. So in honor of SFC Porterfield's (first female Sergeant of the Guard) service, and at her request, the schedules were aligned for the first all-woman changing of the guard as part of her last walk." [3]

Affirmative Action

The need to address the imbalance of the last 400 years is a crisis of conflicting theories, ideas, and solutions. Affirmative Action programs were a catalyst for institutional and systemic change to increase diversity representation and yield numerical increases of diversity nationwide.

In March 1961, President John F. Kennedy issued Executive Order 10925 which created the Committee on Equal Employment Opportunity, mandating projects financed with federal funds take Affirmative Action to ensure that hiring and employment practices were free of racial bias.

In September 1965, President Lyndon Johnson issued Executive Order 11246 establishing requirements for non-discriminatory practices in hiring and employment on the part of U.S. government contractors. It remains today, amended and further strengthened over the years, a significant safeguard protecting the rights of workers employed by federal contractors, approximately one-fifth of the entire U.S. labor force, to remain free from discrimination based on their race, color, religion, sex, disabilities, or national origin. [4]

The goal of Affirmative Action programs was to solve the discrepancy in representation, thus representation became both the problem *and* the solution. Affirmative Action is an outcome-driven methodology that provides measurable and quantifiable results. It is designed to impact exclusion and to promote numerical representation of previously excluded groups. Affirmative Action is fundamentally remediation.

According to professor and author Louis Menand, "The reason we have affirmative action is that we once had slavery and Jim Crow and redlining and racial covenants, and that we once had all-white police forces and all-white union locals and all-white college campuses and all-white law firms.

"The paradox of the Civil Rights Movement is that out-lawing racial discrimination made it harder to remediate its effects. Once we amended the Constitution and passed laws to protect people of color from being treated differently in ways that were harmful to them, the government had trouble enacting programs that treat people of color differently in ways that might be beneficial. We took race out of the equation only to realize that, if we truly wanted not just equality of opportunity for all Americans but equality of result, we needed to put it back in. Our name for this paradox is Affirmative Action."[5]

Ironically, a country that promotes individuals creates a solution for groups, yet does not consider the factor of individuals. The solution proposed in America has been the Separate but Equal doctrine since *Plessy v. Ferguson* in 1896, despite having been overturned in 1954 in *Brown v. Board of Education,* ordering the end to school segregation.

If an institution evaluates talent on an individual basis and determines there is a bias, certain groups may not be represented in the organization. Instead of expanding the criteria for evaluating individual talent, the hurried solution became quantifiable group representation, assuming included groups demonstrated qualifications and capabilities as individuals, while excluded groups were not evaluated on the same criteria. They were instead selected by representational quotas. The need to fix things quickly and easily oftentimes results in more complicated problems than originally existed.

Representation of all qualified groups can exist only if all groups are included in the criteria for participation. If representation is the measurement of equality, then representation must be the solution; hence, our conundrum.

Exclusion is an absence of representation due to bias and discrimination, with quantitative results, whereas the procedures of bias and discrimination are qualitative. If one defines the problem solely as representation, then *quantification* of solutions is reasonable, but if one defines the problem as bias and discrimination, then the solution lies in the *qualitative* procedures to secure representation.

This Affirmative Action solution resulted in the inevitable outcry of "reverse discrimination," a term defined in the Supreme Court of the United States in June 1978 as "providing greater opportunities for minorities which came at the expense of the rights of the majority."[6]

Separate but Equal

The creation of Ethnic Studies programs was initially an educational solution to the omission of people of color in U.S. History books and school curriculum. Instead of redesigning the curriculum model, the solution to exclusion was to create a Separate but Equal exclusion system. Inclusion requires the expansion of the criteria for participation.

A predicament created by Ethnic Studies is that white males are excluded in this program and typically see it as a "politically correct" option to satisfy women and people of color, thus diminishing its academic credibility. Sometimes white males who are interested are not well received by the Ethnic Studies minority participants, resulting in two programs of exclusion, U.S. History with its missing information, and Ethnic Studies without its dominant culture representation, dividing rather than uniting us.

More specifically, African Americans learn about African Americans, Asian Americans learn about Asian Americans, and women learn about women. All students are required to learn about the contributions of Europeans in U.S. History, but only non-Europeans are required to take an additional course to learn about their existence and contributions to America. Efficacy of Ethnic Studies courses is based on the educational climate where it is being taught and the culture of intersectionality within the community.

The term misinformation implies deception and premeditated exclusion; if we reframe the issue as missing information, we can explore potential solutions, rather than debating cause and effect. That said, misinformation about cultural practices and lived experiences does exist in the reteaching of history through critical race counterstories.

Ethnic Studies programs were created to remedy the missing and misinformation regarding the existence and roles of women, people of color, and others in the development of America. Ethnic Studies are not separate versions of U.S. History, but rather the transitional component of missing information necessary to understanding America's multicultural journey to the present. Ethnic Studies programs are a bridge to the inclusion of all, an incremental and transitional evolution in education, not the ultimate solution to the problem of exclusion.

Ethnic Studies can result in the creation of side roads for solving the problem of exclusion instead of utilizing inclusion as the critical factor for information, education, and equity. Without addressing the omissions and overhauling the institutions and systems themselves, we end up with Separate but Equal. Separate but Equal solutions to exclusion result in additional constructs of exclusion. The previously included are excluded from the new solution, and the previously excluded groups are now included in their exclusionary model.

America never anticipated an increasingly diverse population becoming significant contributors to its domestic economy and necessary for continued success globally. Thus, the United States does not have a history of promoting systemic changes to benefit excluded groups without legal interventions.

Since we consistently proceed without a plan or strategy, we have sought quick fixes rather than systemic solutions for excluded groups which resulted in two major forms of accommodations: (1) Affirmative Action strategies to measure equity success through a representation formula for the excluded groups; and (2) Separate but Equal models such as Jim Crow laws for institutional segregation, Ethnic Studies for U.S. History, and Special Education for physically and mentally challenged students. Our propensity to resist systemic change for inclusion has perpetuated the inequities and increased the divide among excluded and included groups. Yet we continue to create Separate but Equal solutions to exclusion. Separate systems are never equal. Separate but Equal will always result in two excluded groups, not just the original one.

Brown v. Board of Education from December 9, 1952 – May 17, 1954 changed the nation. The Supreme Court overturned decades of jurisprudence when it ruled that state laws denying equal access to education based on race violated the equal protection clause of the 14th Amendment, overturning the Court's 1896 ruling in *Plessy v. Ferguson,* the legal basis for "Jim Crow" laws by upholding the Separate but Equal doctrine, thus segregated schools. *Brown* changed public education in the United States and paved the Civil Rights Movement that took shape in the 1960s and continues today. Thurgood Marshall, in *Brown v. Board of Education,* offered the benchmark "Equal means getting the same thing, at the same time, and in the same place." [7]

"The Social Progress Index," based upon research of Nobel-winning economists, is a collection of 50 metrics of well-being such as nutrition, safety, freedom, the environment, health, education, to measure the quality of life in 168 countries worldwide. "The United States, despite its immense wealth, military power and cultural influence, ranks 28th in the world." The index places the United States behind significantly poorer countries, including Estonia, Czech Republic, Cyprus, and Greece.

The measurement of prolonged systemic inequities is illustrated by the fact that the United States ranks number one in the world in *quality* of universities, but 91st in *access to quality* basic education, perpetuating the cycle of inequality of basic education, resulting in diminished opportunities to continue education at university level. The United States leads the world in medical technology, yet we are 97th in *access to quality* health care.[8]

Equal Opportunity in Education

White flight to the suburbs resulted in Detroit Black communities becoming ghettos. The NAACP represented Vera Bradley and other parents living in Detroit in a

1967 lawsuit alleging that Michigan maintained a racially segregated public school system due to policies isolating Black families, who, because of racially discriminatory housing practices, were excluded from the suburbs where white families fled to avoid integration of schools.

In *Milliken v. Bradley*, the Supreme Court rejected a desegregation plan. The Court left Detroit to desegregate itself. In dissent, Thurgood Marshall observed, "The Detroit-only plan has no hope of achieving actual desegregation. . . . Instead, Negro children will continue to attend all-Negro schools. The very evil that *Brown* was aimed at will not be cured but will be perpetuated." [9]

Proposition 209, Affirmative Action Amendment of 1996, was introduced to address the misperceptions of preferential treatment of African Americans and Latinx Americans in the quest for increased diversity representation in higher education. The rationale for Proposition 209 was eliminating preferential treatment or granting of preferences based on race, sex, color, ethnicity, and national origin in public employment, education, and contracting.

California embarked on this Affirmative Action strategy to increase diversity enrollment in the college and university systems. The numerical representation was increased in the name of diversity; however it was supposed to be a short-term remedy, not a permanent solution to the problem. Since it did not appear to include a termination timeline, the outcries of "reverse discrimination" were the response to this strategy for artificial diversity representation. The uproar, primarily by white students and their supporters, resulted in the Proposition 209 repeal of Affirmative Action in November

1996, enabling California to adopt a constitutional ban on race-based and sex-based Affirmative Action.

This rejection of perceived preferential treatment for people of color completely ignored the historically rampant preferential treatment for wealthy students, children of influential donor parents. Wealthy white Americans have always enjoyed unwritten benefits throughout our social, educational, economic, and political systems. The year 2020 saw multiple indictments of wealthy white individuals for bribing universities to accept their children.

There is no denying that the passage of Proposition 209 resulted in a significant decline of applicants and acceptance of African Americans and Latinx students, drastically reducing these populations from enrollment in California State and University systems.

California is currently facing the same discrepancies in diversity representation as those necessitating the original Affirmative Action solutions in the 1980 –1990s. However, the conditions are not the same so the solution cannot be the same. Instead of an artificial fix like Affirmative Action, the solution to the representation problem is a systemic overhaul to ensure equity in access to public education.

A topic of national discourse is "freedom of school choice," the underlying cause of which is "unequal education opportunities." The issue needs to be reframed to "how to provide equality of education for all students?"

Briefly summarized, the cycle is thus: unequal housing opportunities are used to create the foundation for funding neighborhood schools, calculated upon the community tax base. Wealthier neighborhoods enjoy wealthier schools, better facilities, better equipment, better resources, better teachers, and better-prepared students. Better-prepared students in public schools have more opportunities for higher levels of education, which results in more college graduates and better opportunities for better employment, which affords better housing opportunities in better economic neighborhoods. The cycle repeats.

A 2014 lawsuit filed by Students for Fair Admissions against Harvard University highlights the issue of inadequate solutions to equity and natural diversity representation. The lawsuit was filed by more than a dozen Asian American students who applied and were rejected for admission. They contend that they were passed over by Harvard, who favored less academically qualified racial and ethnic minorities.[10]

Harvard responded that it uses finely-calibrated factors to produce a spectrum of diversity; not only of race, but income, ideas, geographic origin, and talents. This is a veiled attempt to justify their discretion to select applicants with severely biased criteria, such as "dean's or director's list," which included children of wealthy donors receiving special consideration in admissions.

This provided a view of discrimination that preceded Affirmative Action programs and required a new institutional model for equity and diversity to ensure a process that will achieve fair goals and outcomes. If diversity representation were a legitimate factor for admission to Harvard, then what were the measurable criteria for determining which individuals, not groups, were qualified?

While institutional racism has a cumulative effect, it impacts not only individuals but groups, as well. The Catch-22 in this form of institutional racism is the fact that *groups* are negatively affected by lack of access to public education, then subsequently rejected on *individual* merit at the university level. For example, Black and Latinx students, as groups, have limited access as a result of lower economic public schools, yet their potential for advancement at higher education institutions is evaluated on individual learning experiences and capabilities compared to students who received a higher level of academics at their more privileged and well-funded public schools. One cannot experience inadequate education as a *group,* then be required to compete with other individuals who were afforded higher educational opportunities as an *individual.*

CHAPTER 9

Who versus *What?*

*R*ecognition of racism in the criminal justice system as a whole, specifically focused on policing institutions throughout the country, resulted in a clamor for accountability. Questions to be asked are whether every individual in the police forces of America is racist or whether the working cultures created in police forces are racist.

These questions reveal the essence of the *Who* versus *What?* dichotomy of racism. Individual racism is a *Who* phenomenon, whereas institutional or systemic racism is a *What* phenomenon. Addressing individual racism analyzes the opportunity, logic, and benefits of changing individuals' beliefs and behaviors. Prejudice, bias, and bigotry are all elements of individual racism and require an entirely different strategy from that of eliminating institutional or systemic racism.

The *Who* solution to racism requires an individual change of one's beliefs, prejudices, and discriminatory behaviors. The *Who* problem is regarding individuals, and the *What* problem is regarding institutions and systems. For example, the current call for modifying police training is a *Who* solution to a *What* problem. This strategy will not eliminate institutional or systemic racism. It may potentially make some individuals more sensitive to inequitable treatment of minority groups but does not require any change in their behaviors or policing methodologies.

The 2021 Derek Chauvin guilty verdicts on three counts for the murder of George Floyd[1] reverberated across the nation, mandating the accountability of the individual police officer, separate from the institution itself, and placing the onus on administration for massive [systemic] police reform. With every citizen capable of recording live testimony to abuses of the badge, individual officers will no longer be impervious to the will of the people, and will be held accountable for equality and justice before the law.

The *Who* versus *What?* analytical tool is not limited to racism, and is applicable to any major change or institutional advancement assessment. Case in point, technological advancement is a *What* factor, yet how it affects change becomes a *Who* casualty. There is no denying the functional benefits of technology; still, we must always measure the advancement positives against the costs to human lives and livelihoods and address the loss of employment and self-worth. Unemployment is much more complex than solely an economic dilemma.

The World Economic Forum predicted in 2018 that technology will develop 58 million more jobs than it loses by 2022, with continued growth after the fact. Mechanizing work does not necessarily remove jobs; it instead shifts the job market to be highly tech maintenance based.

What are the impacts of technology reducing the need for human participation and production? If a new machine can replace the work of five individuals, then what will those five individuals do for employment? If an individual has worked twenty-five years as a toll taker on the Golden Gate Bridge in California, how will they earn income when the local government establishes "FasTrak" transponder capabilities, eliminating the need for toll takers?

FasTrak and the privatization of the carpool lane is one of the greatest inequity issues the San Francisco Bay Area is facing. With the rising cost of housing in the Bay Area we see an increase in commuters who now have to pay to use a lane to get to work on time or risk being late and losing their job, or have to wake up significantly earlier to beat the traffic, leading to greater stress on the workforce.

Not all technology harms society. The introduction of cameras on cell phones enabled individuals to record and share police actions towards Blacks in America. Blacks raised their voices against police brutality towards them in dire desperation for years without remedy. With new technology *What*, we are equipped with visual evidence of needless abuse of our citizens *Who*. The brutal homicide of George Floyd inflamed the critical relevance of the Black Lives Movement. Photos and video from the January 6 insurrection on the Capitol were instrumental in the investigation.

The Supreme Court historically made decisions based on their interpretation of the Constitution and legal precedent. That fact represents the *What* part of the equation. The Supreme Court now rules the legitimacy of the Affordable Care Act, voting rights, *Roe v. Wade*, presidential election results, all of which affect millions of Americans, the *Who*, in these grave decisions.

PART FOUR

Post-2020 and Future America

CHAPTER 10

Government Dysfunction

The structures for governance designed by the Founders provided accountability by the balance in power of its three branches: Executive (President), Legislative (Congress or the Senate and House of Representatives), and Judiciary (the Supreme Court). This configuration was once an ideal model. American society has changed, and today our government is woefully out of sync. We now have dysfunctional government institutions and systems, as well as individuals and groups willing to manipulate that chaos for power.

The Framers of the Constitution, primarily James Madison and Alexander Hamilton, had raised the concern for the adaptability of the document as the country progressed. Change is necessary and imminent if we are to remain a democratic republic. Senators and Representatives have disavowed their sworn oaths and adherence to the guide rails of the Constitution, undermining the Rule of Law.

The pressures of politics upon the Supreme Court and Federal judges have rendered them unable to perform their most basic function of "Equal Justice Under Law." The partisan selection of Supreme Court and Federal Justices for lifetime conferment has become a battle to leverage the support of a party's ideology. Justices no longer represent the will of the American people. Instead they represent political views of their appointment party and have divided the Courts into a new version of "North versus South," "not conservatives versus liberals, but backward versus forward-thinking." [1]

Political Influences on American Government.

Instead of relying on the most expedient and accessible method for change, *education,* we must instead focus on the most influential venue, which is the *political system.* Our political system has atrophied into a system of unethical dysfunction, with all of its components requiring significant modifications. Following are issues to consider and readdress.

(For more information on this topic, consider *The Politics Industry: How Political Innovation Can Break Partisan Gridlock and Save Our Democracy,* by Katherine M. Gehl and Michael E. Porter; and *Responsible Parties, Saving Democracy from Itself,* by Frances McCall Rosenbluth, Damon Wells Professor of Political Science and Ian Shapiro, Sterling Professor of Political Science, both at Yale University.)[2]

Term limits + qualifications for all federal offices. (1) Term limits for all offices. (2) Competency qualifications, including a test on the Constitution. (3) Age restrictions. We currently have different minimum ages to qualify for serving, Representatives at twenty-five years, Senators at thirty years, and Presidents at thirty-five years. Establish a maximum age limit for all offices. (4) Requiring disclosure of ten years of tax returns will provide financial wealth information to the American people for each public servant in the Presidency, Congress, and the Supreme Court.

Supreme Court. Supreme Court Justices are no longer apolitical, reflecting the will of the people; instead their decisions reflect the political and ideological battles of the day. (1) They should be subject to term limits, as restrict all other public servants. (2) Remove the power to select Supreme Court Justices from Congress; instead, allow the people to select them. Let the Justices represent the American people by being elected, and not be political appointments. No one should be above the law; also no one should *be* the law.

Uniform voting by states in national elections. Democracy requires participation by its citizenry. One vote per citizen. *Not* voting is not a solution; instead it is a quantifiable measure of lack of involvement in the United States, where only 55.7% of eligible voters actually vote. The United States ranks 26th out of the 32 democratic nations in the world.

Campaign Finance Reform. (1) Eliminate corporate funding of individuals. (2) Create a single general election fund for all donors: corporate, wealthy individuals, and ordinary Americans to make their donations. These funds can be equally distributed to each qualified applicant running for offices.

The Electoral College. The Founders created the Electoral College in 1804 as the 12th Amendment to the Constitution because they did not want Congress to select the next President and they did not believe the popular vote had "enlightened statesmen" to make such an important decision.

The Electoral College consists of 538 electors, whereby a majority of 270 electoral votes is required to elect a President. It results in the possibility for a candidate to win specific states, securing 270 electoral votes without winning the majority of individual citizen votes. This results in an undemocratic outcome, a winner without the majority of votes.

There have been five presidential elections where the winner was elected without a majority of the votes of the American people: Democratic-Republican John Quincy Adams in 1824; Republican Rutherford B. Hayes in 1876, Republican Benjamin Harrison in 1888; Republican George W. Bush in 2000; and Republican Donald J. Trump in 2016. Adams lost the popular vote by the smallest margin of 38,149 and won the Presidency. Trump lost the popular votes by the greatest margin to date of 2,868,686 and won the Presidency.[3]

The Filibuster. This simple procedural mechanism allows the minority party to block legislation from advancing in the Senate or severely delay action by debating it at length, offering numerous procedural motions, or any other delaying or obstructive tactics.

A filibuster keeps debate open on a legislative item until the Senate votes to close it. Closing debate requires 60 votes instead of the usual 50. The practical result is that one needs to get 60 votes or bypass the filibuster to bring legislation to a final vote.

The original tactic was a "talking" filibuster, the lengthiest in 1957, when Senator Strom Thurmond, one of the southern Democrats opposed to the Civil Rights legislation, spoke for 24 hours and 18 minutes. Talking filibusters have not been required since the 1970s when the Senate changed the rules to simultaneously permit more than one bill to be pending on the Senate floor. Presently, an emailed *threat* of a filibuster translates to an automatic requirement of a super majority vote of 60 Senators to end a debate.

The filibuster is undemocratic, not in the Constitution, created to protect the minority party in the Senate from being overrun by the majority party, allowing it to block the majority party from passing bills and to prevent an unrestrained takeover of legislation. There is no filibuster in the House of Representatives because rules strictly limit each representative's amount of time on the House floor.

The filibuster empowers the minority to block the will of voters and the American public. The filibuster has been repeatedly weakened over the last 100 years to avoid total gridlock and dysfunction:

1917 ⋆ Senate instituted a means for officially cutting off debate through a supermajority vote. Before this, there was no means of stopping a filibuster at all. With this change, cutting off debate required two-thirds of all senators, usually 67.

1974 ⋆ Senate eliminated the filibuster for budget bills meeting specific requirements, a legislative process called "reconciliation."

1975 ⋆ Senate lowered votes for ending a filibuster from 67 to 60 Senators

2013 ⋆ Senate eliminated the filibuster for federal executive branch appointees and judicial appointments, other than the Supreme Court.

2017 ⋆ Senate eliminated the filibuster for Supreme Court nominees.

Reforming the filibuster is not a radical idea held by fringe leftists. In 2018, reflecting on his presidency, Barack Obama said, "Adding the filibuster … has made it almost impossible for us to effectively govern at a time when you have at least one party that is not willing to compromise on issues." In 2020, Obama again called to eliminate the filibuster, calling it a "Jim Crow relic." A host of liberals, centrists, and even a few conservatives have noted the incredible political dysfunction fostered by the filibuster.

Eliminating the filibuster is easy. It merely requires a simple majority vote in the Senate, and can be done at any time. Notable is a loophole in the called "budget reconciliation" that allows the majority to advance legislation with only a simple majority for legislation that directly impacts government spending or taxes.

Filibuster abuse has resulted in almost insurmountable partisan gridlock and the inability to pass legislation on behalf of the people. There are effectively three options currently available: (1) remove the filibuster from the Senate rules; (2) require the reinstatement of the "talking" filibuster; and (3) invoke the "nuclear option" to require a simple majority of 51 votes to bring closure of the debate time [still allowing for 30 hours of debate time].[3]

The elimination of the filibuster is currently not supported by all Democratic Senators, thus rendering it an impossibility. Reinstatement of the "talking" filibuster, plus requiring all Senate members to be present for the duration, could restrict the abuse. The "nuclear option," more formally "reform by ruling," would be to create a new Senate precedent, standing alongside Senate Rule 22 which can, in certain circumstances, be employed with support from only a simple majority of Senators.

The National Rifle Association (NRA). The NRA has become the strongest and most influential lobbyist in blocking stronger gun control laws. This movement of violence defends its "right to bear arms" quoting the 2nd Amendment of the Constitution. This right has enabled America to become the most heavily-armed country globally; we have 120,413 firearms per 100,000 citizens, more than one weapon per person.

America is number one in fatality, 7.7 per 100,000 citizens, on the opposite end of the continuum from Japan, Singapore, South Korea, and the United Kingdom with virtually 0 deaths per 100,000 citizens. The common denominator in these safe countries is their stringent gun laws. In the United States, 45 of the 50 states have open carry laws, with only California, Florida, Illinois, New York, South Carolina, and the District of Columbia outlawing the public carrying of weapons. We are the only country globally that promotes public sales of military assault weapons, clearly not intended for personal protection, only to kill.[4]

We have the worst rate of gun violence among all developed countries, yet due to the NRA, we cannot regulate weapons. We have killings in nightclubs, public entertainment events, religious facilities, family and neighborhood celebrations, job sites, individual disagreements, and, possibly the most inconceivable of all, the killing of children in public schools. After the mass murder of 58 people at a 2017 concert in Las Vegas, broadcast personality Bill O'Reilly claimed that mass casualties were "the price of freedom."[5]

The National Rifle Association was established in New York in 1871 to improve marksmanship skills if citizens were called upon to fight in another war and to promote the British sport of elite shooting in tournaments. Rifle clubs sprang up across the country. In 1931, the NRA supported federal legislation limiting concealed weapons, possession of arms by criminals, the mentally ill, children, and requiring background checks. A faction of the NRA later broke away from sports and opposition to gun control to form a political action committee focused on "gun rights."

Leaders of the NRA endorsed Movement Conservative presidential candidate Ronald Reagan and the Republican platform opposed to federal registration of firearms in 1980. After an attempt to kill Reagan, shooting and paralyzing his press secretary James Brady, Representative Charles Schumer (D-NY) introduced the Brady Handgun Violence Prevention, known as the Brady Bill, requiring background checks before the purchase of guns. While NRA member Reagan endorsed the bill, the NRA spent millions to defeat it.

The Brady Bill finally passed in 1993, and the NRA promptly sponsored lawsuits in nine states to strike it down. The Supreme Court declared parts of the measure unconstitutional in 1997. By 2000, the NRA was one of the three most powerful lobbies in Washington and began backing Republican candidates, including more than $30 million on Trump. The right to own and carry weapons symbolized the Republican party's individual liberty ideology.

A 2005 law granted gun manufacturers immunity from liability claims for deaths resulting from their products. However, the Connecticut Supreme Court ruled that Remington could be held legally responsible for the marketing that made the AR-15 rifle the weapon of choice for mass shooters. In July 2021, the bankrupt Remington Arms Company offered to pay $33 million to settle claims against them by victims of the Sandy Hook school massacre, leaving 20 first-grade children and six faculty dead. The settlement reached in February 2022 was $73 million for nine families.[6]

America's Two-Party System

George Washington's prescient farewell address warned against hyper-partisanship: "The alternate domination of one faction over another, sharpened by the spirit of revenge, natural to party dissension, which in different ages and countries has perpetrated the most horrid enormities, is itself a frightful despotism." His successor, John Adams, was also concerned that "a division of the republic into two great parties . . . is to be dreaded as the great political evil."[7] The Framers thought that by separating powers across competing institutions, a majority party would never form.

Originally called Democratic Republicans, the Democratic Party is the oldest voter-based political party globally and the oldest existing political party in the United States. They were founded in the early 1830s, known as the party of the "common man," standing for individual rights and state sovereignty.

That party ultimately evolved into a white supremacist organization, endorsing segregation through Jim Crow laws. Democratic President Andrew Jackson passed the 1830 Indian Removal Act evicting 46,000 Indians from the "Five Civilized Tribes" (Cherokee, Choctaw, Chickasaw, Creek, and Seminoles) in The Trail of Tears march to concentration camps, clearing the way for white settlers.

The Republican Party was founded in the 1850s by anti-slavery activists such as Abraham Lincoln, initially espousing free labor, free land, and free men. The Republican Party was associated with civil rights and emancipation, while the Democrats supported southern segregationists, inequality, and racism. Black voters supported the Republican Party from the 1860s to the 1930s. Frederick Douglas said, "The Republican Party is the ship; all else is the sea." [8]

The Democratic Party platform as we know it today appeared during the Franklin D. Roosevelt presidency and the New Deal. It was during this time that Black voters began to switch allegiance from the Republicans to the Democrats. The passage of President Lyndon B. Johnson's Civil Rights Act in 1964 and Voting Rights Act in 1965 solidified the Black voter support for the Democrats. [9]

The Republican Party began to split over the support of Black votes versus southern business votes. It is notable that the first 23 Black congressmen were Republicans and represented the anti-slavery party. However, the parties reversed ideologies, and of the following 140 Black congress members, 131 were Democrats and 9 were Republicans.[10]

By the 1960s through the 1990s, American politics was almost a four-party system with liberal Democrats and conservative Republicans alongside liberal Republicans and conservative Democrats. The post-civil rights movement re-aligned the two parties. "National politics transformed from a compromise-oriented squabble over government spending into a zero-sum moral conflict over national culture and identity. As the conflict sharpened, the parties changed what they stood for. And as the parties changed, the conflict sharpened further. Liberal Republicans and conservative Democrats went extinct. The four-party system collapsed into just two parties."[11]

The Democratic Party represented diversity and cosmopolitan values, and dominated cities. The Republican Party represented traditional values and Anglo Christian identity, and fled cities to flourish in the exurbs. Since 1992, the nation has cycled through two pendulum swings, heightening distinctions between the parties and intensifying partisanship.[12]

Republicans transitioned from Lincoln's party of equality and anti-slavery to today's split between the traditional values of white supremacy, tax cuts benefiting business and the wealthy, and those values of the Party of Trump, essentially terminating Reagan-era conservatism.[13]

These three trends: the nationalization of politics, the geographical-cultural partisan split, and consistently close elections, have increased the divide, forcing both parties into top-down leadership, party discipline and destroying the possibility of bipartisan deal making. Voters now vote for the party, not the candidate. Sorted by geography and cultural values, neither party has the chance of becoming dominant.

Still, that elusive permanent majority promises so much power that neither side will give up.[14]

Our current status breaks the system of separation of powers and checks and balances that the Framers created. The system is no longer one of bargaining and compromise, instead that of capitulation and stonewalling.

Congressional stonewalling leads presidents to act by executive order, strengthening the power of the presidency, exacerbating hyper-partisanship, and resulting in more gridlock. Hyper-partisanship intensifies legislative gridlock, thus leaving critical decisions to the judiciary to resolve. Given lifetime tenure, this makes Supreme Court and Federal Jurist appointments even higher stakes. Our two-party system has resulted in winner-take-all elections.

"The most compelling theory based on historical patterns of democratic decline is that hyper-polarization cracked the foundations of American democracy, creating the conditions under which a party could break democratic norms with impunity because winning in the short term became more important than maintaining democracy for the long term."[15]

If unopposed, a possible outcome is more contested elections, more violence, and a collapse into competitive authoritarianism. When partisans see their political opposition not just as the opposition but as a genuine threat to the nation's well-being, support for democratic norms fades because "winning" becomes everything. Politics collapses into a war of "us against them," a kind of "pernicious polarization" that repeatedly appears in democratic collapses around the globe.[16]

Given current trends, with the growing illiberalism of the Republican Party and its shift from democratic norms, reversing the Trump era requires something radical: breaking up the Democratic and Republican parties.

According to Matthew Shugart, professor emeritus of political science at the University of California, Davis, there are three major political divisions in the United States: (1) the Democratic/Republican which splits the country roughly 50/50; (2) the capitalist/socialist pits people on the far left, such as Senator Bernie Sanders (I-VT) [who proposes a wholesale overhaul of the economic system] against everybody else, left or right; and (3) the most salient division is the democratic/authoritarian split on the right. [17]

"On this one, the pro-democratic segment extends all the way from the leftmost large-d Democrats to somewhere near the middle of the Republican Party," Shugart wrote. On the other side is the Trumpian wing of the GOP, which has "shown itself to be completely willing to set aside democracy, and even to promote/tolerate political violence, in order to advance its political agenda." [18]

Ending two-party politics is not mere fantasy. Nothing in the Constitution requires a two-party system. The Fair Representation Act is a bill (1) creating multi-member House districts in states with more than one representative, (2) requiring those districts be drawn by independent commissions to minimize gerrymandering, and (3) allowing voters to use a ranked-choice voting system. [19]

"It will make the House much more representative of the American people and make it a more stable body." It will transform elections from a winner-take-all model to one of proportional representation in which parties win seats in proportion to the number of votes their members receive. [20]

In a multiparty democracy multimember districts would fracture the Democratic and Republican parties. Multimember districts would allow voters to follow their consciences rather than choose the lesser of two evils. It would enable the moderate forces within the GOP to reclaim the party from the authoritarian faction.

Researchers who study elections have found that government works better in multiparty proportional systems. Voter turnout is higher because voters have a greater choice among viable candidates. People report greater satisfaction with the government. Partisan debates are less hostile. Minority populations get better representation.[21]

It also creates more stability in government. In our current system there are wild swings back and forth as Democrats and Republicans trade control of Congress and the White House, undoing the previous majority's work each time. Coalitions shift over time, but they're unlikely to shift that dramatically in a proportional system.[22]

A proportional system's main benefit is the quality of representation, a better match between constituent opinion and government action. Initiating such a system does not require a constitutional amendment, but it would need the support of a majority of members of Congress. If Congress does not take further steps, moderate Republicans will soon be shut out of power altogether. "This is your last chance to save your party from acolytes of Trump who would rather burn the system down than pass sensible moderate and conservative policies that are popular with the electorate," said Shugart.[23]

CHAPTER 11

A Presidential Election,
November 3, 2020

"Those who can make you believe absurdities can make you commit atrocities." — Voltaire

Some of us mistakenly concluded we had arrived at a post-racial era in America after having elected President Barack Obama in 2008. During his two-term presidency, we were unaware of the severe and visceral threats to white supremacy, insults to white privilege, and the zero-sum equation of equality in America, where every gain of minority inclusion was perceived as a loss to the dominant majority who excluded them.

President Obama's very existence threatened an entire population of mostly conservative white evangelical Christian Republicans, who were easily whipped into a racist, xenophobic, and misogynistic backlash of voters, effectively resurrecting the 1960s "Southern Strategy" playbook of Richard Nixon and Barry Goldwater. They rallied political support among white voters across the South by leveraging their racism and fear of people of color, emphasizing law and order, states' rights, their thinly-veiled appeal to racists, and a rebuttal of the Civil Rights Movement.

Both parties had atrophied, becoming hatefully partisan. Political debate took place online, ever more frantic and desperate and paranoid. Nationalism and white supremacy were on the rise in the United States and Europe. Party politics abandoned any national purpose, such that subsequent

presidential nominees from both parties declared large portions of American citizenry unworthy of their attention and
beneath their contempt.[1]

Conservative white supremacists were vengeful after
eight years of government under an African American president. Anglo Christian evangelicals ignored their religious
beliefs to vote for Trump and his platform of "America First,"
the KKK slogan, wielding a white supremacy agenda. The
2016 election resulted in an unprecedented four-plus years
of dismantling our civil norms, institutions and systems — of
Democracy itself — through lies, punitive retaliations, transactional negotiations, autocratic demands of absolute loyalty
above law, and abuses of the American balances of power in
government. Trump divided the country, split the Republican
party in two, and launched a post-truth era in America.

Zero-sum white supremacists were especially sensitive
to accommodations of Blacks and people of color in demographics, immigration, voting, and the 2020 Census. Many
white individuals are not conscious of their racist beliefs, and
reactions to these non-white gains are subliminal.

Such was the framework for the second coming of Mark
Twain's "Gilded Age of America," that era glittering on the
surface but corrupt underneath. The late 19th century was a
period of greed and guile, of rapacious Robber Barons, unscrupulous speculators and corporate buccaneers, shady business practices, scandal-plagued politics, and vulgar display. By
any measure, it was the worst of times.

Trump was not a solution to the problem of America's
cultural decline, instead a symptom of it. Jefferson wrote in
the Declaration of Independence "Let facts be submitted to a
candid world," founding a nation appealing to truth.[2]

The repeal of the Fairness Doctrine in 1987, the demise of the daily newspaper, and the plummeting decline of broadcast television news resulted in a rise of unregulated channels such as the Rush Limbaugh radio show and cable networks such as CNN, MSNBC, and Rupert Murdoch's Fox News channel. We now have an alt-right news media without regulation of factuality and truth, currently purveyors of post-truth era lies and conspiracy theories, along with a complementary array of alt-right social media platforms.

Between the September 11 attacks in 2001 and the election of Trump fifteen years later on November 9, 2016, the United States lost its way. Its party system fractured, the Press were banished, and all three branches of government disintegrated. The nation appeared on the verge of a civil war as if the American experiment had failed and Democracy was in danger of dying.[3]

What happened is not unique to the United States. The wave of nationalism and strong man authoritarian rule, disenfranchising voters, appears to be a global phenomenon.[4] *When bombarded with lies, repeatedly, the purpose of the lie is not to persuade one to believe the lie; it is to persuade one to doubt everything.*

All limits of reality based upon facts, truth, and accurate information were destroyed. Lying became normalized, truths reclassified as misinformation, disagreeable facts became "fake news." Conspiracy theories were legitimized. Most dangerous and damaging, the American Press were labeled enemies of the people. These critical power plays established a cult of alternative reality.

QAnon, a disproven and discredited American far-right conspiracy theory group infiltrated the Republican Party with two elected officials to the House of Representatives in 2016, along with at least a dozen Republican congressional candidates for the mid-term elections in 2022.

The 2020 Presidential Election ripped the social fabric of the country and created the most serious ideological divide since the American Civil War. We are experiencing a modern-day war, not between the North and the South over the slavery issue, but between a cult of autocracy and reality. We are living in a moment of lies versus truth, corruption versus honesty, and critically, demagoguery versus Democracy.

Former President Trump refused to accept the democratic election of Joseph R. Biden, Jr. as the 46th President of the United States. Trump instead declared his victory "by a landslide," and flooded Courts with over 50 baseless lawsuits lacking evidence to support his accusations of fraud and cheating with electoral ballots. Trump was the only president in American history not to participate in the peaceful transfer of power.

One of the fundamental values of America is respect for and adherence to the Rule of Law, despite the reality that wealthy people and white people tend to have a different rule of law than poor people and people of color. That notwithstanding, once the Rule of Law is shattered, what remains?[5]

When asked how history would view the Trump administration, Justice Ruth Bader Ginsburg's response was two words, "An aberration." [6] However, in November 2021, the International Institute for Democracy and Electoral Assistance, based in Stockholm, Sweden, released its 2021 report on "The Global State of Democracy."

"Democracy is at risk," the report begins. "Its survival is endangered by a perfect storm of threats, both from within and from a rising tide of authoritarianism. . . . The world is becoming more authoritarian as nondemocratic regimes become even more brazen in their repression and many democratic governments suffer from backsliding by adopting their tactics of restricting free speech and weakening the rule of law."

The report identifies the United States as one of the democracies that is "backsliding," that has "experienced gradual but significant weakening of Checks on Government and Civil Liberties, such as Freedom of Expression and Freedom of Association and Assembly, over time."

"The United States, the bastion of global democracy, fell victim to authoritarian tendencies itself, and was knocked down a significant number of steps on the democratic scale."[7]

A Confederate Flag Flew in our Nation's Capitol on January 6, 2021

The nonpartisan Coup D'état Project at the Cline Center of the University of Illinois, which analyzes and categorizes political violence, determined that the storming of the Capitol "was an attempted coup d'état, an organized, illegal attempt to intervene in the presidential transition by displacing the power of the Congress to certify the election."[8]

The unprecedented coup attempt exposed uncomfortable realities which we have long denied. Compare the lax management of policing and minuscule presence of Capitol Police during the *forewarned* attack, in contrast to the vast number of police, national guard, and military presence at the peaceful Black Lives Matter protest in Washington, D.C. summer 2020. This disparity is a clear demonstration of the essence of white privilege.

A second shocking reality was the sheer number of police, fire, current and ex-military who participated in the unlawful attack on the Capitol. Trump enabled dormant feelings of white supremacy to surface not only among his Republican Party sycophants but also among individuals sworn to protect America from violence and lawlessness.

According to historian Christopher Haley, "Nearly a century after the Tulsa Race Massacre, the country would again see another white mob attack. On January 6, 2021, pro-Trump supporters stormed the U.S. Capitol. People watched in shock as insurrectionists scaled the Capitol build-ing, encouraged by the 45th president of the United States. The insurgents—including military veterans, police officers and elected officials—broke through police barricades and poured into the rotunda. They walked through the labyrinth of the Capitol hunting for members of Congress and threat-ening to kill the Vice President and Speaker of the House.

"Historians conclude that in order to understand our country's racial divide and the attack on the Capitol, one must understand the racial tensions that led to the Red Summer of 1919. 'What we are facing within the racial ten-sion that revealed itself in 2020, coupled with the Pandemic, is sadly, ironically and tragically the result of what happened 100 years ago during 'Red Summer,' when there was a slew of race riots in American cities.'

"Haley said there is a correlation between the January 6, 2021 storming of the U.S. Capitol and the events that led to Red Summer. 'I think the correlation is that the people rioting were white supremacists, Nazis or anti-Semitic. They carried Confederate flags. That certainly links itself to those persons during Red Summer who hated the progress of

African Americans and politicians. It would be stretching it to say there is no correlation.'"[9]

* * * * *

*A*mericans endured the chaos of 2020 facing racial division, political strife, a reeling economy, poverty, all while grieving deaths from the Coronavirus Pandemic and the untimely losses of human and civil rights pioneers John Lewis, Ruth Bader Ginsburg, and others. With a country divided and a battle to maintain our democratic way of life, we prayed for tranquility, and looked to new leadership to heal and to unify our great nation once again, a call for what Abraham Lincoln pleaded as a search for our better angels. Jill Lepore in *These Truths, A History of the United States,* wrote:

> The American experiment has not ended. A nation born in revolution will forever struggle against chaos. A nation founded on universal rights will wrestle against the forces of particularism. A nation that toppled a hierarchy of birth only to erect a hierarchy of wealth will never know tranquility. A nation of immigrants cannot close its borders. And a nation born in contradiction, liberty in a land of slavery, sovereignty in a land of conquest, will fight, forever, over the meaning of its history.[10]

President Obama urged Americans "to choose our better history," a longer, more demanding, messier, and, finally, more uplifting story. A nation cannot choose its past. It can only choose its future.[11]

In February 2021, a bipartisan group of more than 400 mayors across the country begged Congress to provide aid to cities. Mayors and governors have to make government work and thus are often more practical and less ideological than national lawmakers.

The mayors noted that "American cities and our essential workers have been serving at the frontlines of the ongoing COVID-19 Pandemic for nearly a year" without direct federal assistance. Because cities and states cannot borrow to cover budget shortfalls, they look to the federal government, which *can* borrow, to tide them over in times of crisis.

During the previous administration that aid was not forthcoming. Left with no choice, local governments had to cut nearly a million local government jobs. Direct, flexible aid to cities would help suffering families and fuel a recovery, the mayors said, as well as enable cities to vaccinate people.[12]

President Biden's $1.9 trillion American Rescue Plan, was signed into law on March 12, 2021. The legislation supported ordinary Americans as well as cities and states, aided the country through the economic downturn caused by the Pandemic, and marked a change in government, the likes of which have not been seen since President Franklin Delano Roosevelt's New Deal in the 1930s. With the expansion of the child tax credit, relief is projected to reach approximately 27 million children, to cut child poverty in half, "a new lifeline to the middle class." It targeted money to low-wage earners, particularly to women and people of color. Biden used the national government not to cut taxes, which favors those with wealth, but rather to support working families and children. Not one Republican in the House or Senate voted to support this bill.[13]

This bold move rested on the idea that the federal government must help manage the economy. Republicans abandoned this idea to the Reaganomics of the 1980s, even today insisting that tax cuts benefiting the wealthy and private enterprise are the keys to a secure economy. Trump's Tax Cuts and Jobs Act of 2017 amending the Internal Revenue Code of 1986[14] benefited only wealthy corporate leaders, enabling them to invest their increased profits from tax cuts into stock buybacks, driving money upward, while proving punishing to the average American.

In an address regarding the Pandemic and vaccine distribution logistics, President Biden asked Americans to do their part by getting the vaccine and helping friends and family get theirs. "If we do all this, if we do our part, if we do this together, by July the Fourth, there's a good chance you, your family and friends will be able to get together in your backyard or your neighborhood and have a cookout and a barbecue and celebrate Independence Day. After this long hard year, that will make this Independence Day something truly special." He also said, "The government isn't some foreign force in a distant capital . . . It's us. All of us. We the people." [15] *Our aforementioned all-American 4th of July Independence Day BBQ!*

On March 7, 2021 fifty-six years after Bloody Sunday on the Edmund Pettus Bridge, President Biden signed an executive order "to promote voting access and allow all eligible Americans to participate in our democracy." Biden's Executive Order to Promote Voting Access,[16] directed federal agencies to assist states under the National Voter Registration Act, improve and modernize Vote.gov, increase federal employees' access to voting, analyze barriers to voting for people with disabilities, increase voting access for active-duty military and other overseas voters, provide voting access and education to citizens in federal custody, and establish a Native American voting rights steering group.

He also called upon Congress to pass the For the People Act, making it easier to vote, and to restore the Voting Rights Act, renamed the John R. Lewis Voting Rights Act for the man who went from his days in the Civil Rights Movement to serve seventeen terms as a Representative from Georgia, bearing his Bloody Monday scars until his death July 17, 2020.[17]

CHAPTER 12

Post-2020 Enduring Challenges

Truth, Misinformation & Social Media. The emergence
of social media in the early 2000s paved the way for increased
social connection beyond one's immediate circles. Initially
meant to allow friends and families to interact and share life
events from anywhere around the globe, its unprecedented
growth was unaccompanied by proportionate regulations.
Between 2005 and 2019, use of social media by adults alone
grew from 5% to almost 80%.[18] However, a lack of trans-
parency and accountable governance meant that the reach
of social media would extend unchecked and vulnerable to
manipulation, resulting in increased ease of dissemination
of misinformation.

In 2020, journalist Maria Ressa wrote "In a battle for
facts, in a battle for truth, journalism is activism. Disinformation is how you transform a democracy. This is death by
a thousand cuts. The same thing is happening in the United States. I think the goal of influence operations or information operations is to seed it, repeat it, incite hate . . . and
change the way real people think, and that impacts the real
world. This is happening all around the world. That's what the
research has shown us, that's what the data shows us."

The Nobel Peace Prize 2021 was awarded to two jour-
nalists, Maria Ressa of the Philippines, and Dmitry Muratov
of Russia, both of whom had to endure the threats and political persecution of their respective autocrats, Rodrigo Duterte
and Vladimir Putin, while battling online disinformation and
attacks on the press. [19]

A 2021 leak revealed that Facebook, (renamed "Meta" for the metaverse) had been used for a variety of motives, including allowing foreign powers to hone political pressures in the U.S. around the 2016 and 2020 elections.[20] Additionally, the site allowed for the spread of false medical information during the pandemic which resulted in a greater number of COVID-related deaths,[21] and even provided a platform for the insurrectionists to plan out their attack on the nation's capital on January 6, 2021.[22]

Further, Facebook/Meta has been linked with cases of mental health deterioration, drug dealing, human trafficking, ethnic violence, and more, but has only addressed some of these issues when whistleblowers brought them to the public eye.

Facebook/Meta owned Instagram and WhatsApp, for a total of three of the top six social media platforms on the planet. YouTube was the second most used platform, and has even fewer regulations than Facebook/Meta does. Coupled with the knowledge of irresponsible institutional management, one can see why social media is a problem that persists and amplifies other challenges faced in the United States today.

Black Lives Matter. (BLM) was founded in 2013 in response to the acquittal of Trayvon Martin's murder by the police. It is a political and social movement advocating non–violent civil disobedience protest against police brutality and racially motivated violence against Black people. A global organization in the United States, United Kingdom, and Canada, its mission is to eradicate white supremacy and to help build local power to intervene in violence inflicted on Black communities.[23]

The tragic 2014 police murders of Eric Garner in July, Michael Brown in August, and 12-year-old Tamir Rice in

November fueled the wave of Black Lives Matter protests in Ferguson, Baltimore, Chicago, and New York.

Breonna Taylor in March, and George Floyd in May, 2020 fomented a second wave of protest during the summer in cities across the country and around the world. A cumulation of murders at the hands of local police galvanized a multicultural nation to protest and seek the perpetually deferred justice for African American communities.[24]

Black Lives Matter exemplifies the existence of an excluded group, and is protesting the reality of being constant targets of police violence, invisible to equal protection of the law, and unvalued in their loss of life. BLM does not imply that white lives do not matter, nor that Black lives are more important, yet zero-sum white supremacists interpret Black Lives Matter as devaluing white lives. They do not believe Blacks are of equal value and try to disguise their superiority with the response "All Lives Matter." All Lives Matter reflects the individual belief that equality and inclusion already exist for everyone.

The challenge for America today is (1) to educate individuals who are included to comprehend the plight of groups who are excluded and to agree that their quest for equity is legitimate and just; and (2) to recognize and judge the excluded as individuals rather than groups. The barrier to this accomplishment lies in the cost benefit to the included for assisting the excluded. This is the crux of the issues of white privilege and white supremacy.

In September 2020 the Mayor held a national press conference to address the civil lawsuit between the Breonna Taylor family and the city of Louisville, Kentucky. In his speech, the Mayor confirmed the damage that the Taylor family and the Black community of Louisville had suffered at the hands of the police department and claimed responsibility for the tragedy.

The city of Louisville took a giant step by accepting responsibility and created a meaningful precedent for change. It became a model for other American cities to emulate, to bring justice and institutional change to racially despondent communities.

The Taylor family received a $12 million settlement. Changes to the police department included (1) a subsidized housing credit for all officers residing in the communities they serve, (2) a weekly two-hour community service by police officers in African American communities, and (3) the addition of social and mental health workers to the police force to assist in defusing and managing serious mental health situations. In January 2021, two of the police officers involved in the Taylor shooting were fired.[25]

In March 2021 the Minneapolis City Council voted unanimously to approve a $27 million settlement with the family of George Floyd, the largest ever awarded in the state of Minnesota. "That the largest pre-trial settlement in a wrongful death case ever would be for the life of a Black man sends a powerful message that Black lives do matter and police brutality against people of color must end," said the Floyd family attorney. It was but "one step" on the journey to justice. "Mr Floyd's death was a catalyst for reckoning on race and bias." Floyd family lawyers argued that the city had been negligent for failing to train its officers proper restraint techniques and for not dismissing officers with poor track records. Derek Chauvin served 19 years on the police force and had received dozens of complaints.[26]

This rampant race-based violence has created a sense of futility and a vote of no confidence among some groups of Blacks. *The Week,* September 2020, noted: "A group of 19 Black families has purchased 97 acres of land in Georgia on which to build a pro-Black city. Founder Ashley Scott says she and her co-investors see a need to build a thriving haven for people of color. The new city, Scott says, will be a place where Black people can be a village again, be a tribe again."[27] Secession from a failing Union is a questionable Separate but Equal solution. (See "The Black Wall Street Massacre" in the Omissions and Erasures of Chapter 2.)

Charles M. Blow shared a similar solution in *The Devil You Know.* "The proposition is simple. Black descendants of the Great Migration should return to the South from which their ancestors fled." By concentrating their political power in major Southern cities, Black Americans affect actual social change. "The mission begins with the states, which are the true centers of power in this country, and as such control the lion's share of the issues that bedevil Black lives: criminal justice, judicial processes, education, health care, economic opportunity and assistance."

Blow maintained, "If the Great Migration hadn't happened, and those Black people had remained in the South until the passage of the Civil Rights Act of 1964 and the Voting Rights Act of 1965, it is possible that African Americans would dominate the politics of the Deep South. They could control or be the driving force in electing as many as twelve U.S. senators. Black people could control or form the majority influence for as many as ninety Electoral College votes."[28]

The New York Times published a story about Stacie Marshall on July 4, 2021, titled "Her Family Owned Slaves. How Can She Make Amends?" Marshall inherited a 300-acre farm in Georgia and then learned that her family owned seven people.

Marshall discovered the 1860 County Slave Schedule listing seven people under the name of her great-great-great-grandfather W.D. Scoggins, described only by their ages, genders, and race: 30-year-old male; 35-year-old female; 32-year-old male, 6-year-old female; 4-year-old female; 2-year-old female, and 5-month-old male, all Black.

She consulted Matthew Raiford, a Gullah Geechee organic farmer working the coastal land his ancestors acquired after they were emancipated from slavery, who has become a friend and adviser.

A second upsetting revelation was that W.D. Scoggins acquired the family's original tract of land in an 1833 lottery that awarded confiscated Creek and Cherokee land to white people, with portions of the Trail of Tears not far from her farm. "So you figure out that you got stolen land that had the enslaved put on it, and your family benefited off that for a lot of years," said Raiford, "Now you have to have two different conversations. It gets complicated real fast."

Should the descendants of slave-owners be held responsible for that wrong? What can they do to make things right? What will it cost? "I don't have a lot of money, but I have property.... How am I going to use that for the greater good, and not in like a paying-penance sort of way but in an it's-just-the-right-thing-to-do kind of way?"

She went to her father's best friend, Melvin Mosley, who founded Harmony Baptist Church. "Let's say that's the water under the bridge. You didn't do anything wrong." "In all of our families, Black or white, there are some generational things that are up to us to break," he told her. "And when we break it, it is broken forever."

"Father in heaven," he prayed, "we ask you just to continue to give her the courage and the desire to break the chain of racism, Lord." "People aren't looking for a handout," Mrs. Mosley told her. "We just want justice in all of the things that are going on. It's hard to explain it to a white person, but if you're a Black person you understand."

Jeremy Marshall is a partner in his wife's antiracist work. He compares financial reparations to carbon offsets for guilt-racked white people. "It's like, 'I'm not going to change my life, but tell me a dollar amount that would absolve me of guilt,'" he said. "That kind of transaction, whether it's about the environment or racial inequality, is not going to create change." [29]

Anti-Asian American Violence. The attack on Asians is one with a long history in America, from the Asian Exclusion Act of 1875, the Chinese Exclusion Act in 1882, President Franklin D. Roosevelt's Executive Order 9066 in 1942 and unconstitutional incarceration of 120,000 Japanese, the Korean War in 1950–1953, and the Vietnam War in 1961–1975. Asians have endured cruel racial epithets, hateful malignments, physical attacks, lynchings, and murders for centuries. [30]

Former President Trump fueled anti-Asian sentiment with his racist attacks on the Chinese throughout 2020 using discriminatory rhetoric such as Kung Flu, Wuhan Virus, or the Chinese Virus, inflaming the false notion that Asians were responsible for the spread of the Coronavirus Pandemic. He tapped white supremacists' dormant hatred of Asian foreigners.

The Pandemic put Asian Americans at heightened risk of verbal and physical attacks. Stop AAPI Hate, a national coalition addressing anti-Asian discrimination, racism, and xenophobia, reported 3,800 accounts of anti-Asian hate incidents between March 2020 and February 2021, a time when Asian-American businesses (many of them first-generation immigrant-owned, therefore at a disadvantage when applying for bank and government loans) were already suffering tremendous economic losses.[31]

Of the 3800 reported anti-Asian racist incidents, most were against women. There is an intersectional misperception that (1) both Asians and women, and (2) Asian women, who are sexually fetishized, are easy targets. Youth and the elderly are also vulnerable prey. [32]

A common stereotype is that all Asian students are great in math and science and poor in sports. The assumption is that Asian Americans are well-behaved hardworking overachievers who make it to the highest levels of success, that Asians don't need any help, and that they don't require further examination of how their race faces discrimination. Asians have always been perpetual foreigners. These perceptions can lead to resentment. Resentment can lead to hate.[33]

Originating in the 1960s during the rise of social movements addressing the U.S. war in Vietnam, the environment, racial and gender equality, the portrayal of Asians as the "model minority" myth was "a way to discredit the claims of African Americans who were seeking racial and economic justice and demanding massive structural overhauls in American society." A primary criticism of the stereotype is that it drives a wedge in the long history of cross-racial solidarity between Black and Asian American communities." [34] Both communities are systemically deemed divergent from the white cultural norm, thereby "othered." [35]

Many Asians joined the protest to support the Black Lives Matter movement, yet at the same time felt that they were excluded from the racial discourse. They were angry and alienated by the surge of anti-Asian discrimination. They worried about the shootings of Asian women in Atlanta, Georgia, felt isolated, vulnerable, and frustrated that Asian Americans seem left alone to deal with this fundamental racism.[36]

Racist violence represents only the tip of the iceberg. Due to the twisted logic of racists who see them as an enemy, Asians are targeted as scapegoats. Throughout history white Americans have felt animosity toward Asians for usurping their jobs, particularly along the West Coast of California, and lashed out periodically lynching and eradicating entire Asian enclaves to quell their racist competitive rages.

In the early 1980s, unemployment was its highest since World War II and inflation was in double digits. "Japan Inc." threatened not only Detroit manufacturing but also New York real estate. White flight had emptied the great metropolis that once stood for industrial progress and imported cars became a hated symbol of foreign encroachment. [37]

In 1982, the American auto industry was in a downturn, and mass layoffs erupted as Japanese import cars increased competition. Michigan, home to America's Big Three: Ford, Chrysler, and GM, was suffering decline, and anti-Japanese sentiment had risen since Pearl Harbor. Many Americans blamed the Japanese for the ailing U.S. auto industry.

Vincent Chin was 27 years old, working, and engaged to be married. On June 19, 1982, celebrating his bachelor party with friends at a club, witnesses recalled 43-year-old Chrysler foreman Ronald Ebens, mistaking Chin as Japanese, shouting, "It's because of you motherf***ers that we're out of work."

Ebens and his 22-year-old stepson Michael Nitz, who had lost his job at Chrysler, followed Chin and friends out of the club, grabbing a baseball bat from Ebens' car. Chin ran. Eben and Nitz drove around the neighborhood in search. When they found him, Nitz held Chin while Ebens repeatedly struck Chin in the head with his baseball bat.[38] Two off-duty Highland Park police officers witnessed the beating.[39] Before losing consciousness, Chin whispered to his friend, "It's not fair." He lapsed into a coma, died four days later, and was buried the day after what should have been his wedding day.[40]

On March 16, 1983, Circuit Judge Charles Kaufman ruled the murder an outcome of a barroom brawl, found Ebens and Nitz guilty of manslaughter, fining each $3,000, $780 in court costs, three years' probation, and released them. In defense of his light sentencing, Kaufman said, "These aren't the kind of men you send to jail. . . . We're talking about a man who's held down a responsible job for 17 or 18 years, and his son is employed and is a part-time student. You don't make the punishment fit the crime, you make the punishment fit the criminal."[41]

Although deeply affecting frightened Asian Americans in Detroit (if it could happen to Chin, it could happen to anyone of Asian descent), the murder didn't make national news until the trial judgment. Kin Yee, President of the Detroit Chinese Welfare Council, argued that the sentences amounted to "a license to kill for $3,000 provided you have a steady job or are a student, and the victim is Chinese." [42]

Judge Kaufman's lenient sentencing enraged the Asian American community across the nation. Activist Helen Zia, Asian American lawyers, and community leaders created American Citizens for Justice (ACJ). ACJ allied with other diverse groups, churches, synagogues, and Black activists, to protest Kaufman's sentencing. Stewart Kwoh, co-founder of the Asian Pacific American Legal Center (APALC), read about the sentencing in *The Los Angeles Times.* APALC was the only out-of-state co-counsel to the ACJ, who co-wrote an investigative report aimed at calling federal authorities' attention to the crime.[43]

The FBI investigated the case and the DOJ pressed charges in *United States v Ebens*. Ebens was found guilty of federal civil rights violations and sentenced to 20 years in prison. The jury found Nitz not guilty of civil rights violations, ostensibly because he did not say anything racial. Ebens appealed, and a Cincinnati jury found him not guilty of depriving Chin of his civil rights. Ebens and Nitz did not serve one day in jail for their actions.[44] Vincent Chin became the precedent for prosecution of crimes against Asian Americans under the federal hate crime law.

The Vincent Chin case was pivotal for (1) sparking the Asian American victims and civil rights movement; (2) leading to the formation of American Citizens for Justice; (3) revealing the latitude judges had in sentencing, resulting in the Supreme Court and Congress mandating minimum sentencing guidelines; and (4) displaying the sensitive nature of changing a venue, which may alter the outcome of a trial.

The Vincent Chin case led Asian American leaders to found a national organization to advocate for all Asian Americans. APALC, the Asian Law Caucus (ALC), and the Asian American Legal Education Defense Fund (AALDEF) collectively founded the National Asian Pacific American Legal Consortium in 1991, now called the Asian American Justice Center.

When offered a job at *The Detroit News*, author Paula Yoo was asked by her Asian American journalist friends, "Are you afraid to go live in Detroit because of Vincent Chin?" She responded, "You know, being Asian American in this country, we're often alone. We're often the only one in our high school or the only family on our block because for many, many decades, we have been a very small part of the percentage of the population. So being an Asian

American in this country is very lonely. I've been very lonely my whole life." [45]

The anxiety of many Asian Americans could be mitigated if they shared a more powerful group identity and felt a greater sense of solidarity and unity. "Black people identify strongly as Black, but Asians tend not to have strong identity. A lot of Asians are not that sure where we belong. We don't have a strong group voice." However, the Vincent Chin case resulted in changes in the legal and judicial systems and also inspired an entire generation of younger Asians to become involved as activists, writers, and lawyers, going into politics, trying to effect policy change. "Our voice has been raised, our stories, our history, our contributions have been raised." [46]

Witnessing the xenophobia and violence towards citizens in our communities was particularly disheartening in California's San Francisco Bay Area, Oakland, and San Jose, known for its diversity and commitment to inclusion, equity, social justice, and the birthplace of ethnic studies programs that proliferated across that nation. However, this was not solely an American occurrence. Human rights groups in France, Australia, Brazil, South Africa, and Russia reported similar stories.[47]

In January 2021 President Biden signed the Memorandum Condemning and Combating Racism, Xenophobia, and Intolerance Against Asian Americans and Pacific Islanders in the United States, denouncing the Trump administration's discriminatory sentiments directed at the Asian American and Pacific Islander (AAPI) community, and guiding the Justice Department on its response to the burgeoning number of anti-Asian racist incidents.[48] Addressing the root cause of the violence requires education, expanded civil rights protections, and restorative justice models. The memorandum focused on hate *incidents* rather than hate *crimes*, which are a police issue, allowing for a more holistic approach to combat racism against Asian Americans in public streets, transit, private businesses, and other settings.

Systemic white supremacy is the root of anti-Asian violence, the ideological perpetrator of the recent violent assaults. Asians have been attacked since their arrival in the 19th Century and will forever remain foreigners in the eyes of white supremacists.

White America created the "Yellow Peril" stereotype that continues to kill Asians. Anti-Asian violence is not a single event in time, more a recurring pattern when social anxiety reaches a certain unbearable level. Since the Vincent Chin tragedy, hundreds of lives have been taken, "nameless people of color are killed twice: once by murder, and again by a racist judicial system." [45] The lives of people of color simply aren't worth as much as a white person's life.

The heightened anti-Asian sentiment and violence witnessed between 2020 and 2021 were due to a confluence of factors, including poverty, homelessness, mental health, and financial struggle, all of which were exacerbated by the Pandemic, as well as by the dormant racism and xenophobia unleashed by the former president's racist remarks.

HSS *Improving Cultural Competence* claims "Most literature suggests that poverty and its consequences, including limited access to resources, increase stress and vulnerability among individuals who may already be predisposed to mental illness. Often, theoretical discussions explaining a significant relationship between mental illness and socio-economic status suggest a bidirectional relationship in which stress from poverty leads to mental illness vulnerability and/or mental illness leads to difficulty in maintaining employment and sufficient income."[49]

Racism has become so pervasive and normalized in America that some hate-driven anti-Asian attacks have been committed by African Americans, Latinx, and Muslims. However, the AAPI reported attacks are perpetrated primarily by whites, unlike the sensationalized minority-on-minority incidents portrayed in the news and social media. *Do not assume the individual represents the group.*

The Governor of Illinois signed the Teaching Equitable Asian American History Act (TEAACH) into law in July 2021, mandating Illinois schools to teach Asian American History. Co-sponsor of the legislation, State Representative Gong-Gershowitz, said, "Asian American history is American history. Yet we are often invisible. . . . Empathy comes from understanding. We cannot do better unless we know better. A lack of knowledge is the root cause of discrimination and the best weapon against ignorance is education." [50]

White Privilege and Superiority. Anglos have always been the majority population in America, yet their demographic reflects numerous factors including age, place of birth, parental and family influences, economics, education, literary preferences, peer socialization, political affiliations, religious and ethnic cultural influences, multicultural experiences, languages beyond English, and travel outside of white majority countries.

Privilege is a form of entitlement without awareness. The privileges are inherited systemically by being the criteria of inclusion in the Constitution. The gift of inclusion is a lack of recognition of, and *non*-concern for, one's skin color and the resultant benefits due to that single factor.

According to U.S. Department of Health and Human Services, socioeconomic status is used as a category similar to class, the difference being that socioeconomic status is a more flexible and less hierarchically defined concept. Socioeconomic status in the United States is related to many factors, including occupational prestige and education, but is primarily associated with income level. It affects culture in several ways, most important through a person's ability to access resources, opportunities, and accumulate material wealth. Discrimination and historical racism have led to lasting inequalities in socioeconomic status.[51]

Journalist Laura Cathcart Robbins wrote "Privilege, though, is not confined to money or pedigree. Although most people generally think of privilege as socio-economic, that's just one of many categories. Of course, there is white privilege, but there's also colorism. Colorism, favoring light-skinned people over darker skin tones, is real and present in both Black and white communities.

"We could also talk about gender privilege (men still get paid more than women for the same jobs, and that's a fact). There's cis-hetero privilege, educational privilege, ZIP code privilege, right-handed and able-bodied privilege, age, hair privilege."[52]

Superiority is a complex issue of an inherited individual or group belief or bias engendered by the devaluation of Blacks for electoral counting purposes in the Constitution and transferred from generation to generation as proof of their inferiority and an inherent white superiority. This is also the group of "zero-sum mentality."

To quote scholar Frances Lee Ansley, "By 'white supremacy' I do not mean to allude only to the self-conscious racism of white supremacist hate groups. I refer instead to a political, economic and cultural system in which whites overwhelmingly control power and material resources, conscious and unconscious ideas of white superiority and entitlement are widespread, and relations of white dominance and non-white subordination are daily reenacted across a broad array of institutions and social settings."[53]

Majority is a neutral term, simply the numeric demographic of the largest ethnic, cultural, and racial group in America. The previous two issues reflect the broad dimension of beliefs, attitudes, and behaviors towards people of color, especially Blacks. This is a transitional, perhaps transactional, statistic for America moving forward into a more multicultural nation. Demographic projections indicate whites will become a minority population in America within the next twenty-five years.

It is important to remember that white supremacy and systemic exclusions are not limited to Black Americans, but affect all people of color, women, the physically challenged, LGBTQ, non-Christian evangelical religious groups, the aged, ill, poor, essentially any individual not appearing to reflect the dominant Anglo caste.

One approach to unity is by educating white citizens of their dominant caste status, and the concomitant institutional racism. White privilege requires recognition and acceptance of dehumanizing beliefs, attitudes, prejudices, and behaviors towards Blacks, people of color, and other "different" individuals. This is essentially retroactive programming, requiring that the recipients of negative programming, while not all innocent victims, accept their unconscious participation in a vicious cycle of their sense of superiority.

The phenomenon was witnessed when CNN news anchor Anderson Cooper, who had just had a son, was discussing the concept of white privilege with distinguished Harvard and Princeton professor Dr. Cornel West. When West asked whether he was prepared for *"the conversation,"* Cooper was stunned and confused by the question. *"What conversation?"* West responded, *"The one where you educate your son how to respond to a police officer when he will be pulled over for a traffic violation."* In the gestalt of that moment, Cooper experienced what white privilege meant. He confessed to Dr. West it had never entered his mind that he would have to do so, and was forthright enough to admit that he finally understood the depth that privilege accords to whites in America. He realized it meant never having to think about one's own life in direct comparison to the life of African Americans or any other ethnic minority, never having to think about the serious consequences of racism in America.[54]

A comprehension of the pervasiveness of white privilege naturally segues into other issues of what it is to be "American" when one is distinctly representative of one's nation of origin, biracial, or multiracial. Every non-white family needs to prepare its children for the micro-aggressions and other forms of racism they will experience in their communities, in schools, on public transit, and in the workplace.

In March 2021, parents in Mancelona, Michigan, were in an uproar over an 11th-grade high school teacher's unprecedented writing assignment titled "White Privilege and Whiteness." Conceived to engage discussion in class, it instead resulted in a debate around town. White students and parents brought it to the Board of Education.

"When you have a school system where a large majority is white, it's a very uncomfortable situation," one parent said. "It's a very uncomfortable situation because you would have to sit there, take a look at yourself, understand you have privilege, you don't have to feel bad for it, and then use that privilege to help make life better for other people." Some parents felt that receiving this assignment could be difficult for students in the room who aren't white. "I think it's a form of bullying. I think you're singling out people for bad things," another parent stated. "You're singling out the most innocent people in our society."

The Board of Education said they are open to curriculum changes. "Mancelona Public Schools leaders remain committed to reviewing curriculum and materials to ensure that we are doing our part to promote learning and understanding and being representative of the community we serve, adjusting as needed while doing so with an open mind," stated the Mancelona Public Schools Board.[55]

When spontaneous, lessons like these may be welcomed as opportunities to engage in discussions and emotional responses. First-person learning for change is not always smooth or comfortable, but absolutely necessary and consequential.

Critical Race Theory. According to the American Bar Association, *A Lesson on Critical Race Theory* (CRT) is a practice of questioning the role of race and racism in society that originated in the legal academy and spread to other fields of scholarship. "It critiques how the social construction of race and institutionalized racism perpetuate a racial caste system that relegates people of color to the bottom tiers. CRT also recognizes that race intersects with other identities, including sexuality, gender identity, and others. CRT recognizes that racism is not a bygone relic of the past. Instead, it acknowledges that the legacy of slavery, segregation, and the imposition of second-class citizenship on Black Americans and other people of color continue to permeate the social fabric of this nation." Its central tenets include:

(1) "Recognition that race is not biologically real but is socially constructed and socially significant. It recognizes that science (as demonstrated in the Human Genome Project) refutes the idea of biological racial differences. Race is the product of social thought and is not connected to biological reality.

(2) "Acknowledgment that racism is a normal feature of society and is embedded within systems and institutions, like the legal system, that replicate racial inequality. This dismisses the idea that racist incidents are aberrations but instead are manifestations of structural and systemic racism.

(3) "Rejection of popular understandings about racism, such as arguments that confine racism to a few 'bad apples.' CRT recognizes that racism is codified in law, embedded in structures, and woven into public policy. CRT rejects claims of meritocracy or 'colorblindness.' CRT recognizes that it is the systemic nature of racism that bears primary responsibility for reproducing racial inequality.

(4) "Recognition of the relevance of people's everyday lives to scholarship. This includes embracing the lived experiences of people of color, including those preserved through storytelling, and rejecting deficit-informed research that excludes the epistemiologies of people of color."

While challenging white privilege, CRT exposes deficit-informed research that ignores and often omits, the scholarship of people of color. Some of the most blatant illustrations of racism being replicated through systems are visible within the education system. Limitations of legal interventions to date include the following manifestations of racial inequality in education:

(1) "The predominance of curriculum that excludes the history and lived experiences of Americans of color and imposes a dominant white narrative of history; (2) Deficit-oriented instruction that characterizes students of color as in need of remediation; (3) Narrow assessments, the results of which are used to confirm narratives about the ineducability of children of color; (4) School discipline policies that disproportionately impact students of color and compromise their educational outcomes (such as dress code policies prohibiting natural Black hairstyles); (5) School funding inequities, including the persistent underfunding of property-poor districts, many of which are composed primarily of children of color; and (6) The persistence of racially segregated education."[56]

Students are not being taught Critical Race Theory as a course in schools. CRT is a frame of reference recommending the inclusion of facts, information, and history previously omitted by racist educational institutions.

Twenty-First Century Demographics. America no longer reflects our Anglo landed-gentry Founders. By 2030 one out of three children will be Latinx. By 2045 people of color will exceed the white population, becoming the majority in America, people of color at 50.3%, whites at 49.7%. Mixed racial populations of 310,000 in 1970 increased to over 2,340,000 in 2008. By 2035 the sixty-five years and above senior population will outnumber their children by 49 to 95 million.[57] This shift to a majority of people of color will likely increase dormant zero-sum insecurity among the white population.

The 2020 Census. This decennial tabulation was created to count every person living in the United States and its five U.S. territories. The results determine the number of seats each state has in the House of Representatives and are also used to draw congressional and state legislative districts. Census data is the foundation of our democratic system of equality and representation. Gerrymandering is the process whereby a political party manipulates voting boundaries and districts to benefit themselves and to adversely affect their rival political party.

Over the next decade, lawmakers, business owners, and many others will base critical decisions on the 2020 Census data. The census indicates where communities need schools, hospitals, roads, public works, and services for families, older adults, and children. The results also inform how hundreds of billions of dollars in federal funding will be distributed to state and local education agencies (LEAs or school districts), allocating funds to special education grants, Title I grants, the National School Lunch Program, and the Head Start preschool program.[58]

Our 2020 Census is an example of a critical database having been compromised by politics and deliberate distortion of data. The methodology to collect data was flawed by guesstimating the number of residents in poor and minority households rather than counting them, and the truncated timeline which reduced the quantity and accuracy of the data. Facts and truth must prevail over politics and manipulation.[59]

Truth to Power. Until the current threat to American democracy: the replacement of truth and fact with hatred, lies, and conspiracy theories is managed and resolved, we all live in peril of loss of our freedoms and safety.

Our two-party system is at an impasse over truth and reality, with a weakened and wounded democracy at stake. As Quaker civil rights leader Bayard Rustin urged in 1942, now is the time to "speak truth to power." President Barack Obama awarded Rustin the Presidential Medal of Freedom posthumously in 2013.[60]

President Biden continued to fulfill his promises to the American people. The Biden administration was the picture of diversity, not merely by representation, but by demonstration of the value and utility of its cabinet members' unique capabilities, experiences and contributions to their government posts.

In June 2021, the Senate confirmed Muslim American Zahid Quraishi as federal judge, a much belated appointment considering Muslims have been part of America since the early days of African enslavement in the 1600s. The Senate confirmed Quraishi, the son of Pakistani immigrants and veteran of two tours of duty in Iraq, to the U.S. District Court for the District of New Jersey.[61]

The Senate also confirmed Judge Ketanji Brown Jackson to the U.S. Court of Appeals for the District of Columbia Circuit. This post is generally seen as a stepping stone to the Supreme Court. Biden has suggested he would appoint a Black woman to the Supreme Court.[62]

In his joint address to Congress in 2021, President Biden sent an unequivocal message of significant progress for public support of diversity: "To all transgender Americans watching at home, especially the young people, You're so brave. I want you to know your President has your back."[63]

This is diversity in America.

Conclusion

James Baldwin wrote "There are days—this is one of them—when you wonder what your role is in this country and what your future is in it. How, precisely, are you going to reconcile yourself to your situation here and how you are going to communicate to the vast, heedless, unthinking, cruel white majority that you are here. I'm terrified at the moral apathy, the death of the heart, which is happening in my country. These people have deluded themselves for so long that they really don't think I'm human. And I base this on their conduct, not on what they say. And this means that they have become in themselves moral monsters." [1]

Raoul Peck, author of *James Baldwin Was Right All Along*, wrote "Baldwin's words are forceful and radical; he punctures the fantasy of white innocence and an infantile attitude toward reality. He understood that there is an extraordinary capacity for denial in this country, even when confronted with evidence and logic. His was a deep knowledge of the white psyche, which he thought was marred with immaturity.

"First, the genocide of Native Americans: 'We've made a legend of a massacre,' he said, which is a narrative 'designed to reassure us that no crime was committed' and propagated by Hollywood's 'cowboys and Indians' stories. Then, the haunting legacy of slavery: 'I can't say it's a Christian nation, that your brothers will never do that to you, because the record is too long and too bloody. That's all we have done. All your buried corpses now begin to speak.'

"Why can't we understand, as Baldwin did and demonstrated throughout his life, that racism is not a sickness, nor a virus, but rather the ugly child of an economic system that produces inequalities and injustice? The history of racism is parallel to the history of capitalism. The law of the market, the battle for profit, the imbalance of power between those who have all and those who have nothing are part of the foundation of this macabre play. He spoke about this not-so-hidden infrastructure again and again: 'What one does realize is that when you try to stand up and look the world in the face like you had a right to be here, you have attacked the entire power structure of the Western world.' And more pointedly: 'I attest to this: The world is not white; it never was white, cannot be white. White is a metaphor for power, and that is simply a way of describing Chase Manhattan Bank.'

"'We've always known that people were subjugated, even murdered in such a way. Men, women, children. None of that is new. And this has been known at the highest level of this country. When Baldwin rhetorically asked himself almost 60 years ago, 'What can we do?,' his answer was devastating: 'Well, I am tired . . . I don't know how it will come about, but I know that no matter how it comes about, it will be bloody; it will be hard.'" [2]

* * * * *

Article 1. Section 2 of the United States Constitution resulted in the subjugation of an entire "race" or caste in our society, along with the mistreatment of other minorities.

I believe we need a revolutionary reset of all America's institutions, from academia to entertainment and sports, finance, the press, and social media. Change is essential. Our current governmental system is broken. There are no intra-system fixes. Constitutional amendments alone will not suffice. Systemic exlusions can be eradicated only through the process of inclusion to achieve equality and justice for all. Systemic change is predicated on individual change. The solution of inclusion can occur only when all individuals have access to truth.

President Obama wrote "We are living through a moment of rapid disruption, in technology and the global economy, in our social arrangements and our environment. Too often, it feels as if our major institutions have failed to respond effectively to these disruptions. And in the breach, we've seen a growing culture of cynicism and mistrust, more division and more bitter conflict.

"The good news is we can reverse these trends, reimagine our institutions, and rebuild our societies in a way that gives more and more people a better life. Around the world and right here in Chicago, there are young people who aren't waiting for someone else to solve big problems. Instead, in the face of sometimes impossible odds, they are rolling up their sleeves and putting down stakes and making a difference, one neighborhood, one school, one community at a time. This coming generation of leaders is the source of my hope."[3]

We are embarking upon an important decade in the marathon where every generation takes the baton and moves forward. They will continue the vehicle of peaceful protest, devise changes to current political infrastructures, and increase political participation to reflect our society today, and to secure justice and equality for all.

Seeing and accepting racism are steps toward the creation of a solution to our current divide. Progress requires learning and understanding the consequences of racism, the will to confront it, and the work towards its eventual eradication.

In 2021 California became the first state to require that all students complete a semester-long course in Ethnic Studies to earn a high school diploma. California Community Colleges and California State Colleges have already offered courses in Ethnic Studies, but will now require completion of a course to receive an Associate or Baccalaureate Degree.[4]

* * * * *

Designs of Omission has introduced you to some of the systematic omissions and erasures of truth in our U.S. History books. It has provided a historical backdrop to racism, immigration, multiculturalism, exclusion, and offered solutions for systemic change and inclusion in America. Hopefully, the information presented will spark a recognition of exclusions and racism, inherent institutional and systemic design flaws, and become a catalyst for discussion, activism, and change.

As immigrants and citizens of America, the rights, responsibilities, and obligations for addressing the past, present, and future are now yours. May you become allies and work together toward change, as individuals, within groups, helping to unify our communities, continuing to strive toward that persistent goal of "a more perfect Union," and a more accurate reflection of "We the People." "We hold these truths to be self-evident." *Veritas liberabit vos.* The truth will set you free.

About the Author

*B*yron Noriyoshi Kunisawa, a *Sansei*, third-generation Japanese American, was born in the Japanese Internment Camp of Topaz, Utah, youngest of four siblings, two boys and two girls. Byron's mother, Shizue, was a single parent with the sole responsibility of raising her four children.

He was the first in his family to go to college and graduated from California State University, San Francisco with a B.A. in Sociology, K-9 teaching credential, and a Masters in Educational Administration (M.E.A).

He was an educator in the Palo Alto Unified School District and in the Cycle 7 Teacher Corps Project to develop teachers for low income communities. He was selected to a National Multicultural Drug Prevention Advisory Board for the National Institute on Drug Abuse (NIDA). He co-founded the NIDA Advisory Board and the San Francisco Multicultural Training Resource Center (MTRC) in 1985. MTRC was awarded the California State Multicultural Aids Prevention Center contract in 1986.

Kunisawa is an internationally recognized consultant and lecturer in the areas of Workforce Diversity, Organizational Development, Multiculturalism, and Systemic Change. His clientele included NASA, CIA, National Science Foundation, Teledyne-Ryan Aeronautical, Bell Communications Research, National Education Association, NOAA, Department of the Treasury, Hewlett Packard, National Forestry Service, City of Vancouver, Canada, United States Football League (USFL), and Ministry of Multiculturalism, British Columbia, Canada.

His work was recognized and awarded by NASA Public Service Award and Medal in 1994. The International Diversity Speakers Association (IDSA) selected Kunisawa as the Outstanding Global Diversity Speaker for 2007 in Mexico City.

After retiring from public speaking, Kunisawa joined a special team of instructors and caregivers at Marin Ventures, a day program for Developmentally Disabled Adults in San Rafael, California, for nearly a decade.

Acknowledgments

It has taken me this long to fully appreciate and acknowledge all of the sacrifices my family made for me to become the first-generation college graduate with a myriad of opportunities for an independent life. *To those I owe a debt of gratitude for enabling my life's journey:*

Shizue Yamashita, matriarch of an interned, impoverished, yet resilient family. As a single parent of four children, she survived the Internment Camps, public racism, poverty, and horrible barriers of discrimination. I am still in awe of how she kept our family together and never appeared down, angry or depressed despite the tragic events and setbacks she was confronted with and forced to navigate alone.

My mother had a great sense of humor and always critiqued my wardrobe with an eye on what she could wear. She loved my Polo down vest, so naturally it became hers, thus she was the only senior wearing a Polo down vest while walking her best buddy Otto, the German Schnauzer.

She was an incredible cook and spent her limited free time reading recipe books and creating her own renditions of Japanese-American comfort food. She was ahead of her time in her beliefs and acceptance of diverse individuals. She had gay and transgender friends who frequented our house, and even gave her Otto for her birthday. I was a Latchkey child before the term was created, but my mother always left us with food and sage advice on not wasting our time, always learning something, and helping others. My brother Ron took that most to heart; he was never present at Thanksgiving or holiday dinners, instead volunteering at shelters and food kitchens for the poor or homeless.

My mom once worked as an assistant in the I Magnin hair salon and relied on tips to buy food and necessities; she always remembered those days and every time we went to a restaurant, reminded us to tip the servers generously. I will never forget the night, after being on her feet at work all day, she took my brother and me on an AC Transit bus to the Oakland Auditorium, to stand in line in order to receive free shoes for Back to School. Mothers Day will always have a special meaning to me, and should be a national holiday.

Her children: Nobu, the eldest and backbone of the family, wanted to be a nurse, but sacrificed her educational opportunities to go to work to help support the rest of us; Reiko, my free-spirited sister was inherited (her mother was my mom's youngest sister who passed away during the Internment Camp process), and a blessed part of our family; Ron, the eldest son, also postponed going to college to help support our family, was far and away the most compassionate and civic minded of us; lastly, myself, the beneficiary and recipient of all their sacrifices.

Nobu's husband and my brother-in-law, Timo, was our guardian angel. Great unassuming gentleman. Their eldest son Wendell reminded me that Timo spelled backwards is Omit. This is only relevant if you knew how quiet and unassuming he was, without needs or requests. I once asked him if he was bothered by anything; his response was "I don't drink instant coffee." Timo was a remarkable person. He was so meticulous about organizing and not wasting that he put tinsel icicles on the Christmas tree one at a time, and removed them the same way, to save and reuse them, reducing trash. He was recycling before there was a term for it. I never heard him complain except once, when his youngest son Keith was hitting so many home runs in Little League that they refused to pitch to him and instead walked him.

Their daughter Debbie and her husband Michael Hill are the remaining foundation of our family. Niece Debbie has embraced the matriarchal role and is the nucleus of communicating important benchmarks and hosting family celebrations. Michael and Debbie are unconditionally supportive and a lifeline to anyone in the family who needs assistance.

Edward O. (Pete) Lee, whose father was Chinese and whose mother was African American, grew up in the segregated south and, through relentless perseverance, survived racism, the Korean War, and obtained a college degree from UC Berkeley. He was a staunch labor leader, high school educator, independent businessman and the most knowledgeable person regarding the politics and utility of Equal Employment Opportunity and Affirmative Action (EEO/AA) in America. He taught me everything about Civil Rights, Affirmative Action, and surviving in a racist society. Pete Lee was the most generous and independent thinking person I am honored to have known. Like so many great thinkers, he was guilty of being too far ahead of their time.

I will never forget Beatrice Jones Ross, my biggest fan and harshest critic, business partner, agent, and incredible friend. She once hired a court reporter to capture one of my presentations. Despite producing many hundreds of pages, no book emerged. Her passing left me with the constant reminder that I had unfinished business. This book allows me to fulfill her final request.

I distinctly remember that, during one of the most difficult times in my life, a breath of fresh air entered, Jeri Carrothers Coakley, who encouraged (actually pestered) me to present my ideas as a book. It was not the right time, despite her having provided me with numerous "How to Write a Book" manuals. I can now send her a copy of that book.

The blessing of my career was the privilege of working at Marin Ventures, a day program for Developmentally Disabled Adults in San Rafael, California. No words can describe the beauty and compassion of this wonderful organization.

Rachel Dondero, my dearest friend, dedicated hours to reviewing the manuscript and provided numerous insightful literary recommendations. Her positive support and encouragement were instrumental to completing this book.

Gil and Aimee Hirabayashi have supported my work throughout my career, particularly my personal theories and solutions for change in America.

Despite her debilitating health, Joan Lee has remained an inspiration and provides unconditional support for the completion of this book.

Travis Li is the catalyst for the development of this book, and a beacon for the hope and future of equality in America.

Lastly, Travis and I would like to acknowledge gratitude to our editor, Stephanie Young, for her brilliant additions and modifications to more than just the body of the book. Beyond her editing, she managed the design, production, printing, and publishing of the book. Thank you.

Bibliography

A Case for Reparations, by Ta-Nehisi Coates, *The Atlantic Monthly*

A Different Mirror, A History of Multicultural America, by Ronald Takaki

Between the World and Me, by Ta-Nehisi Coates

Black Reconstruction in America, 1860-1880, by W.E.B. Du Bois

Caste, by Isabel Wilkerson

Dark Money, by Jane Mayer

Facing the Mountain, A True Story of Japanese American Heroes in World War II, by Daniel James Brown

Notes of a Native Son, by James Baldwin

On Gold Mountain, by Lisa See

Sojourners and Settlers, Histories of Southeast Asia and the Chinese, by Anthony Reid

Stamped from the Beginning: The Definitive History of Racist Ideas in America, by Ibram X. Kendi

The 1619 Project: A New Origin Story, by Nikole Hannah-Jones

The Autobiography of Malcolm X, by Alex Haley

The Constitution of the United States, U.S. Citizenship and Immigration Services

The Devil You Know, A Black Power Manifesto, by Charles M. Blow

The Fire Next Time, by James Baldwin

The Immortal Life of Henrietta Lacks, by Rebecca Skloot

The Souls of Black Folk, by W.E.B. Du Bois

The Sum of Us: What Racism Costs Everyone and How We Can Prosper Together, by Heather McGhee

The Warmth of Other Suns: The Epic Story of America's Great Migration, by Isabel Wilkerson

The Declaration of Independence, U.S.Citizenship and Immigration Services

These Truths, a History of the United States, by Jill Lepore

Un-American, The Incarceration of Japanese Americans During World War II, by Richard Cahan and Michael Williams

Unfinished Business: The Case for Supreme Court Repudiation of the Japanese American Internment Cases, by Peter Irons

Media Resources

A People's Journey, A Nation's Story
The Smithsonian National Museum of African American History & Culture, Washington, D.C.

Asian Americans
A five-hour film series that delivers a fresh perspective on a history that matters today, more than ever. As America becomes more diverse, and more divided while facing unimaginable challenges, how do we move forward together? The intimate personal stories cast a new lens on U.S. history and the ongoing role that Asian Americans have played, PBS.

Go For Broke National Education Center
Defining Courage Exhibition, Los Angeles, California, features a hands-on participatory learning experience teaching the history of Japanese Americans in World War II and its relevance to our lives today.

I Am Not Your Negro
A film by Raoul Peck based on James Baldwin's thirty pages of notes for a book project called *Remember This House,* which was never completed because it was too excruciating to do so. Academy Award nominee 2017.

Slavery and the Making of America | The Slave Experience: Living Conditions for California educators, PBS Learning Media.

Slavery By Another Name
Series challenges one of America's most cherished assumptions: the belief that slavery in this country ended with Abraham Lincoln's Emancipation Proclamation of 1863, PBS.

The 1619 Project
https://www.nytimes.com/interactive/2019/08/14/magazine/1619-america-slavery.html

The African Americans: Many Rivers to Cross
Series chronicles the full sweep of African American history, from the origins of slavery on the African continent to today when America remains a nation deeply divided by race, with Henry Louis Gates, Jr., PBS.

The Economics of Slavery
In the late 1820s, there were 2 million men, women, and children living in bondage in the United States. What was the economic value of slavery to 19th century American life? American Experience series by PBS.

The Six
Documentary film by Arthur Jones tells the story of an international search led by Steven Schwankert for the Titanic's lost Chinese passengers, a tale of survival and dignity in the face of racism and The Chinese Exclusion Act.

Tulsa's "Black Wall Street" Race Massacre, May 31, 1921
https://www.nytimes.com/interactive/2021/05/24/us/tulsa-race-massacre.html

Vincent Who? — The Film
https://www.vincentwhofilm.com/index.php

Waking up Truth (Parts 1-3), by Byron Kunisawa
https://www.youtube.com/watch?v=3G1CFCVYquE
https://www.youtube.com/watch?v=HE6l0tvoN00
https://www.youtube.com/watch?v=2lEhVQZZS-w

Who Killed Vincent Chin?
A documentary film by Christine Choy and Rene Tajima, with interviews with Chin's mother Lily; his killers, Ronald Ebens and Michael Nitz; Judge Charles Kaufman, who sentenced Ebens and Nitz, but did not jail them; witnesses, friends, and the activists who fought for justice for Chin. Academy Award nominee 1989.

End Notes

Copyright Page

* William Caslon, Adobe Caslon font history.
https://www.fonts.com/font/adobe/adobe-caslon/story

Preface

1. Hughes, Langston, *Selected Poems of Langston Hughes: A Classic Collection of Poems by a Master of American Verse*, (Vintage Classics), September 1990.

2. Churchill, Winston: "Tact is the ability to tell someone to go to hell in such a way that they look forward to the trip," *The Daily Sun*, July 4, 2021.

Introduction

1. McLaughlin Eliott C., "How George Floyd's death ignited a racial reckoning that shows no signs of slowing down," *CNN*, August 9, 2020.

2. Shapiro, Ari, "Black Police Officers Reflect On George Floyd Murder, Derek Chauvin Trial. George Floyd's Murder, One Year Later," *NPR All Things Considered*, May 11, 2021.

3. Coates, Ta-Nehisi, "The Case for Reparations," *The Atlantic*, June 2014.

4. Wright, Flonzie. "The Honorable Congressman John Robert Lewis: 'A Soul Giant,'" *Jackson Advocate*, vol. 82, no. 43, Jackson Advocate, 23 July 2020, p. 2A.

PART ONE
The Constitution of the United States is America's Original Sin

1. Speech of John Sherman of Ohio, in the Senate of the United States, May 31 and June 1, 1892. Federal Reserve Bank of St. Louis.

2. *The Declaration of Independence and the Constitution of the United States*, U.S. Citizenship and Immigration Services, M-654 (rev. 07/08)

3. Hansen, Alexander, and Alexander Hansen. "Man, Not Myth: Genius, Human." *Florida Times Union*, July 3, 2016, p. F.7.

4. Auster, Lawrence, "On the Meaning of Racism," excerpt from *The Path to National Suicide: An Essay on Immigration and Multiculturalism*, American Immigration Control Foundation, 1990.

5. "The Constitution: Amendments 11-27," America's Founding Documents, *National Archives*.

6. U.S. Constitution, The Preamble, *The Constitution of the United States*. https://constitution.congress.gov/constitution/preamble/

7. Nittle, Nadra Kareem,"The History of the Three-Fifths Compromise," *ThoughtCo.*, October 30, 2020.

PART TWO
Introduction to
A History of Systemic Exclusion

Chapter 1. Native Americans

1. Locke, John, "The American Enlightenment," *Spotlight At Stanford,* 2021.

2. Diamond, Jared, *Guns, Germs, and Steel, The Fates of Human Societies,* 1997.

3. Sharp, Rachel, "US's longest-serving political prisoner Leonard Peltier says prison is 'torture chamber' amid Covid lockdowns," *The Independent,* January 26, 2022.

4. Harris-Perry, Melissa, interviewed Kent Blansett, the Langston Hughes Associate Professor of Indigenous Studies and History at the University of Kansas on "Native American Activist Leonard Peltier Pleads from Prison Amid Pandemic," *NPR The Takeaway,* January 27, 2022.

5. Cox Richardson, Heather, "The Department of the Interior's New Face, Deb Haaland represents a reckoning with the fossil fuel industry–and our history of mistreating indigenous people," *Notes from an American,* March 17, 2021.

6. Cox Richardson, Heather, "The Department of the Interior's New Face," *Public Seminar.* March 17, 2021.

Chapter 2. African American Racism in America

1. Franklin, Benjamin, *Observations Concerning The Increase Of Mankind, Peopling of Countries, Etc.,* 1755.

2. Coates, Ta-Nehisi, "The Case for Reparations," *The Atlantic,* June 2014.

3. Locke, John, "Two Treatises of Government," *The Federalist Papers,* London 1698.

4. Ibid.

5. "Causes Of The Civil War" | *History Detectives* | PBS video, lesson plans for educators.

6. Hannah-Jones, Nikole, "1619 Project : The New York Times : Free Download, Borrow, And Streaming : Internet Archive". Internet Archive, 2021, https://archive.org/details/1619project. "Nikole Hannah Jones". Nikolehannahjones.Com, 2021, https://nikolehannahjones.com/

A Civil War, Emancipation, and Hatred

7. "Causes Of The Civil War," *History Detectives, PBS,* video, lesson plans for educators.

8. Ibid.

9. The Emancipation Proclamation, *PBS,* Part 4: Narrative, Resource Bank Contents, Teacher's Guide.

Foner, Eric, "Tracing President Lincoln's Thoughts On Slavery," *NPR Fresh Air,* February 21, 2011.

10. Ibid.

11. Coates, Ta-Nehisi, "The Case for Reparations," *The Atlantic,* June 2014.

12. Ibid.

13. Ibid.

14. Robinson, Randall, *The Debt: What America Owes to Blacks,* January 1, 2001.

Post-Emancipation Jim Crow South, 1890–1965

15. "Jim Crow Laws," *American Experience,* PBS. https://www.pbs.org/wgbh/americanexperience/features/freedom-riders-jim-crow-laws/

16. Coates, Ta-Nehisi, "The Case for Reparations," *The Atlantic,* June 2014.

17. Interview with Heather McGhee, *The Sum of Us: What Racism Costs Everyone and, How We can Prosper Together.* 'Sum Of Us' Examines The Hidden Cost Of Racism — For Everyone, NPR, February 17, 2021.

18. Coates, Ta-Nehisi, "The Case for Reparations," *The Atlantic,* June 2014.

19. McGhee, Heather, *The Sum of Us: What Racism Costs Everyone and, How We can Prosper Together,* February 16, 2021.

20. Interview with Heather McGhee, *The Sum of Us: What Racism Costs Everyone and, How We can Prosper Together.* 'Sum Of Us' Examines The Hidden Cost Of Racism — For Everyone, NPR, February 17, 2021.

21. Lewan, Todd, Barklay, Dolores, "When They Steal Your Land, They Steal Your Future," *Los Angeles Times,* December 2, 2001.

22. Coates, Ta-Nehisi, "The Case for Reparations," *The Atlantic,* June 2014.

23. Ibid.

24. Ibid.

The Civil Rights Act, 1964

25. Brown, DeNeen L., "Martin Luther King's scorn for 'white moderates' in his "Letter From A Birmingham Jail," *The Washington Post,* January 15, 2018.

26. Rieder, Jonathan, The Day President Kennedy Embraced Civil Rights—and the Story Behind It," *The Atlantic,* June 11, 2013.

27. O'Donnell, Michael, "How LBJ Saved the Civil Rights Act," *The Atlantic,* April 15, 2014.

28. Fung, Katherine, "181 Black People Have Been Killed by Police Since George Floyd's Death," *Newsweek,* April 20, 2021.

The Red Summer of 1919

29. Higgins, Abigail, "Red Summer of 1919: How Black WWI Vets Fought Back Against Racist Mobs," *History Stories*, July 26, 2019.

30. Ibid.

31. Brown, DeNeen L., "Red Summer: When Racist Mobs Ruled, How a pandemic of racial terror led to the 1921 Tulsa Race Massacre," *American Experience*, February 4, 2021.

32. Coates, Ta-Nehisi, "The Case for Reparations," *The Atlantic*, June 2014.

33. Higgins, Abigail, "Red Summer of 1919: How Black WWI Vets Fought Back Against Racist Mobs," *History Stories*, July 26, 2019.

34. Ibid.

35. Brown, DeNeen L., "Red Summer: When Racist Mobs Ruled, How a pandemic of racial terror led to the 1921 Tulsa Race Massacre," *American Experience*, February 4, 2021.

36. Coates, Ta-Nehisi, "The Case for Reparations," *The Atlantic*, June 2014.

37. Higgins, Abigail, "Red Summer of 1919: How Black WWI Vets Fought Back Against Racist Mobs," *History Stories*, July 26, 2019.

The "Black Wall Street" Race Massacre

38. Parshina-Kottas, Yuliya; Singhvi, Anjali; Burch, Audra D.S.; Griggs, Troy; Gröndahl, Mika; Huang, Lingdong; Wallace, Tim; White, Jeremy; and Williams, Josh, "What the 1921 Tulsa Race Massacre Destroyed," *The New York Times*, May 24, 2021. Interactive article. https://www.nytimes.com/interactive/2021/05/24/us/tulsa-race-massacre.html

39. Ibid.

40. Brown, DeNeen L., "Red Summer: When Racist Mobs Ruled, How a pandemic of racial terror led to the 1921 Tulsa Race Massacre," *American Experience*, February 4, 2021.

41. Parshina-Kottas, Yuliya; Singhvi, Anjali; Burch, Audra D.S.; Griggs, Troy; Gröndahl, Mika; Huang, Lingdong; Wallace, Tim; White, Jeremy; and Williams, Josh, "What the 1921 Tulsa Race Massacre Destroyed," *The New York Times*, May 24, 2021. Interactive article. https://www.nytimes.com/inter-active/2021/05/24/us/tulsa-race-massacre.html

42. Brown, DeNeen L., "Red Summer: When Racist Mobs Ruled, How a pandemic of racial terror led to the 1921 Tulsa Race Massacre," *American Experience*, February 4, 2021.

43. Ibid.

44. Parshina-Kottas, Yuliya; Singhvi, Anjali; Burch, Audra D.S.; Griggs, Troy; Gröndahl, Mika; Huang, Lingdong; Wallace, Tim; White, Jeremy; and Williams, Josh, "What the 1921 Tulsa Race Massacre Destroyed," *The New York Times,* May 24, 2021. Interactive article. https://www.nytimes.com/interactive/2021/05/24/us/tulsa-race-massacre.html

45. Ibid.

46. Ibid.

47. Ibid.

48. Ibid.

49. Brown, DeNeen L., "Red Summer: When Racist Mobs Ruled, How a pandemic of racial terror led to the 1921 Tulsa Race Massacre," *American Experience,* February 4, 2021.

A History of Medical Abuse of African Americans

50. Green, Mike, "Charlottesville's Root Cause: White Supremacy is Undeniably Mainstream American Ideology," *Medium.com,* August 17, 2017.

51. Brown, DeNeen L., "You've got bad blood': The horror of the Tuskegee experiment," *The Washington Post,* May 16, 2017.

52. Skloot, Rebecca, *The Immortal Life of Herietta Lacks,* 2010.

The Poor People's Campaign

53. Strauss Valerie, "MLK: 'If we are not careful, our colleges will produce … close-minded, unscientific, illogical propagandists'," *The Washington Post,* January 17, 2021.

Carson, Clayborne, "Poor People's Campaign, Event: May 12, 1968 to June 24, 1968," *The Martin Luther King, Jr. Research and Education Institute Stanford University.*

Reparations for Descendants of Slavery

54. Logan, Erin B., "L.A. creates advisory commission to study reparations pilot program for some Black Angelenos," Los Angeles Times, June 18, 2021.

55. Jackson Lee, Sheila, Representative, (D.TX) H.R.40 - 116th Congress (2019-2020): "Commission to Study and Develop Reparation Proposals for African-Americans Act."

H.R.40 - 117th Congress (2021-2022): "Commission to Study and Develop Reparation Proposals for African-Americans Act."

56. Hajek, Danny; Martínez, A; and Dickens, Kelley; "A Black family got their beach back — and inspired others to fight against land theft," *NPR,* October 10, 2021.

57. Office of Public Affairs, "Justice Department Announces Multi-Million Dollar Civil Settlement in Principle in Mother Emanuel Charleston Church Mass Shooting, Department Agrees to Settle Allegations Surrounding FBI Actions," U.S. Department of Justice, October 28, 2021.

Monk, John, "Massive $88M settlement reached with families of SC's Charleston church mass shooting," *The State,* South Carolina, October 29, 2021.

58. An Example from our German Ally: "Framework Contract For The Maintenance Of Paving In The Field Of Steles At The Memorial To The Murdered Jews Of Europe [Tender Documents : T445612484]." MENA Report, Albawaba (London) Ltd.,
July 2019.

Chapter 3. The Melting Pot Myth

1. Crossman, Ashley, "What Is the 'American Melting Pot?'" *ThoughtCo,* February 16, 2021.

2. Klein, Christopher, "Remembering Annie Moore, Ellis Island's First Immigrant," *History Stories,* December 28, 2016.

3. Ibid.

4. Harrison, Scott, "From the Archives: Alien Registration Act of 1940," *Los Angeles Times,* February 26, 2017.

5. Yuhasm Alan, "So Muslims beat Columbus to America? They had better get in line," The Guardian, November 17, 2014.

6. Phi, Bao, Vincent Chin: 30 Years Later, *Star Tribune,* June 18, 2012.

7. Noubar, Afeyan, entrepreneur, venture capitalist, philanthropist, born in Lebanon. "2016 Great Immigrants Recipient," *Carnegie Corporation of New York.*

Chinese Immigrants

8. Takaki, Ronald, *A Different Mirror, A History of Multicultural America,* 1993.

9. See, Lisa, *On Gold Mountain,* 1995

10. Reid, Anthony, *Sojourners and Settlers, Histories of Southeast Asia and the Chinese,* 1996.

Japanese Immigrants

11. Takaki, Ronald, *A Different Mirror, A History of Multicultural America,* 1993.

12. Brown, Daniel James, *Facing the Moutain, A True Story of Japanese American Heroes in World War II.*

13. Ibid.

14. Takaki, Ronald, *A Different Mirror, A History of Multicultural America,* 1993.

15. Ibid.

Jewish Immigrants

16. Grubin, David, "The Jewish Amerians, Migration: The Diaspora in America," *PBS* film series. https://www.pbs.org/jewishamericans/watch/index. html

17. Birmingham, Stephen, *Our Crowd, The Great Jewish Families of New York*

18. Takaki, Ronald, *A Different Mirror, A History of Multicultural America,* 1993.

19. Birmingham, Stephen, *The Rest of Us, The Rise of America's Eastern European Jews*

Latinx Immigrants

20. Takaki, Ronald, *A Different Mirror, A History of Multicultural America,* 1993.

21. Sahagun, Louis, "After 36 Days, Chavez Halts Protest Fast," *Los Angeles Times,* August 22, 1988.

22. Nevarez, Griselda, "50 Years Later, Remembering the Delano Grape Strike," *NBC News,* September 26, 2015.

23. Sahagun, Louis, "After 36 Days, Chavez Halts Protest Fast," *Los Angeles Times,* August 22, 1988.

24. Ibid.

25. Lati, Marissa, "The female labor pioneer who battled grape growers and sexism," *The Washington Post,* September 7, 2020.

Filipino Immigrants

26. Trinidad, Elson, "Filipino American History, 425 Years and Counting" | KCET | https://www.kcet.org/socal-focus/filipino-american-history-425-years-and-counting

27. Philippines | migrationpolicy.org. https://www.migrationpolicy.org/country-resource/philippines https://www.migrationpolicy.org/article/filipino-immigrants-united-states-2020

28. "1587 The First Filipino Landing," *Filipino-American History Timeline,* Portland, Oregon.

29. Ibid.

Korean, Vietnamese, and Hmong Refugees

30. Woolley, John and Peters, Gerhard, "Joint Statement Between the United States of America and the Republic of the Philippines," *The American Presidency Project,* October 18, 2003.

31. Kim, Mai Thi, documentary on Operation Baby Lift, 1975, "Daughter from Danang," *American Experience PBS,* April 7, 2003.

32. Ibid.

33. Burnett, John, "Decades After Clashing With The Klan, A Thriving Vietnamese Community In Texas," *NPR Sunday Edition*, November 25, 2018.

34. Yau, Jennifer, "The Foreign-Born Hmong in the United States," *Migration Policy Institute*, January 1, 2005.

Chapter 4. *Shikata ga nai*

1. Brown, Daniel James, *Facing the Mountain, A True Story of Japanese American Heroes in World War II.*

2. Van Tassel, David D., and John J. Grabowski, editors, "Japanese Ohioans," *Ohio History Central.* The Encyclopedia of Cleveland History. Bloomington: Indiana University Press, 1996.

3. Niiya, Brian. "Resettlement in Chicago." *Densho Encyclopedia*, October 8, 2020.

4. Cahan, Richard and Williams, Michael, *Un-American, The Incarceration of Japanese Americans During World War II*, October 2016.

5. Ibid.

6. Lufkin, Bryan, "The fatalistic phrase that every culture has," BBC.com

7. "Japanese American Relocation," *Holocaust Encyclopedia*, April 18, 2019.

8. Cahan, Richard and Williams, Michael, *Un-American, The Incarceration of Japanese Americans During World War II.*

9. "Japanese American Relocation," *United States Holocaust Memorial Museum.* https://encyclopedia.ushmm.org/content/en/article/japanese-american-relocation

10. Trickey, Erick, "Fred Korematsu Fought Against Japanese Internment in the Supreme Court... and Lost," *Smithsonian Magazine*, January 30, 2017.

11. Ibid.

12. Ibid.

13. Chappell, Bill, "It's Fred Korematsu Day: Celebrating A Foe Of U.S. Internment Camps,"*NPR The Two Way.*

14. Irons, Jeremy, *Unfinished Business: The Case for Supreme Court Repudiation of the Japanese American Internment Cases,* a publication of the Earl Warren Bill of Rights Project University of California, San Diego.

15. Lam, Charles "What we can learn from Fred Korematsu, 75 years after the Supreme Court ruled against him," *NBC News*, Feb 17, 2019.

16. Trickey, Erick, "Fred Korematsu Fought Against Japanese Internment in the Supreme Court... and Lost," *Smithsonian Magazine*, January 30, 2017.

17. Ibid.

18. Lam, Charles "What we can learn from Fred Korematsu, 75 years after the Supreme Court ruled against him," *NBC News*, Feb 17, 2019.

19. "Japanese American Relocation," *United States Holocaust Memorial Museum.* https://encyclopedia.ushmm.org/content/en/article/japanese-american-relocation

20. Hirabayashi, Gordon, "Gordon Hirabayashi Interview," October 25, 1983, *Densho Digital Archive*, Steven Okazaki Collection.

21. Ibid.

22. Irons, Jeremy, *Unfinished Business: The Case for Supreme Court Repudiation of the Japanese American Internment Cases*, a publication of the Earl Warren Bill of Rights Project University of California, San Diego.

23. Niiya, Brian, "Resettlement in Chicago." *Densho Encyclopedia*, October 8, 2020.

24. Ibid.

Unfinished Business: The Case for the Supreme Court

25. Irons, Jeremy, *Unfinished Business: The Case for Supreme Court Repudiation of the Japanese American Internment Cases*, a publication of the Earl Warren Bill of Rights Project University of California, San Diego.

26. Ibid.

27. Ibid.

28. Ibid.

29. Cahan, Richard and Williams, Michael, *Un-American, The Incarceration of Japanese Americans During World War II*, October 2016.

No-No Boys

30. Cahan, Richard and Williams, Michael, *Un-American, The Incarceration of Japanese Americans During World War II*, October 2016.

31. "The Nation's Oldest and Largest Asian American/Pacific Islander Civil Rights Organization," The Japanese American Citizens League. https://jacl.org/

32. Cahan, Richard and Williams, Michael, *Un-American, The Incarceration of Japanese Americans During World War II*, October 2016.

33. Brown, Daniel James, *Facing the Mountain, A True Story of Japanese American Heroes in World War II*.

34. Ibid.

35. Anderson, Peter, "Our Japanese Cultural Heritage," Mukilteo Historical Society.

36. Brown, Daniel James, *Facing the Mountain, A True Story of Japanese American Heroes in World War II.*

37. Van Tassel, David D., and John J. Grabowski, editors, "Japanese Ohioans," *Ohio History Central.* The Encyclopedia of Cleveland History. Bloomington: Indiana University Press, 1996.

38. Niiya, Brian, "Resettlement in Chicago." *Densho Encyclopedia,* October 8, 2020.

39. Ibid.

40. Ibid.

41. Ibid.

42. Ibid.

43. Van Tassel, David D., and John J. Grabowski, editors, "Japanese Ohioans," *Ohio History Central.* The Encyclopedia of Cleveland History. Bloomington: Indiana University Press, 1996.

44. Niiya, Brian, "Resettlement in Chicago." *Densho Encyclopedia,* October 8, 2020.

45. Irons, Jeremy, *Unfinished Business: The Case for Supreme Court Repudiation of the Japanese American Internment Cases,* a publication of the Earl Warren Bill of Rights Project University of California, San Diego.

46. Ibid.

47. Cahan, Richard and Williams, Michael, *Un-American, The Incarceration of Japanese Americans During World War II,* October 2016.

48. Hirabayashi, Gordon, "Gordon Hirabayashi Interview," October 25, 1983, *Densho Digital Archive,* Steven Okazaki Collection.

Redemption and Reparations

49. Brown, Daniel James, *Facing the Mountain, A True Story of Japanese American Heroes in World War II.*

50. Irons, Jeremy, *Unfinished Business: The Case for Supreme Court Repudiation of the Japanese American Internment Cases,* a publication of the Earl Warren Bill of Rights Project University of California, San Diego.

51. Ibid.

52. Brown, Daniel James, *Facing the Mountain, A True Story of Japanese American Heroes in World War II.*

53. Irons, Jeremy, *Unfinished Business: The Case for Supreme Court Repudiation of the Japanese American Internment Cases,* a publication of the Earl Warren Bill of Rights Project University of California, San Diego.

54. Katyal, Neal, "Confession of Error: The Solicitor General's Mistakes During the Japanese American Internment Cases," *The Justice Blog*, The United States department of Justice, May 20, 2011.

55. Scarcella, Mike, "In DOJ Speech, Katyal Addresses Japanese Internment Cases," *The BLT: The Blog of Legal Times*, May 24, 2011.

56. Koran, Mario, "California formally apologizes to Japanese Americans for internment camps," *The Guardian*, February 20, 2020.

PART THREE
From Exclusion to Inclusion

Chapter 5. Exclusions: Personal, Cultural, Institutional, and Systemic

1. "Identifying Social Inclusion and Exclusion," *Leaving No One Behind, Report on the World Social Situation 2016*, United Nations, Department of Economic and Social Affairs, Social Inclusion, Chapter 1, November 10, 2016.

2. Mclaurin, V.A., *Stereotypes of Contemporary Native American Indian Characters in Recent Popular Media*, University of Massachusetts Amherst, January 2012.

3. Obama, Barack, *A Promised Land*, March 2021.

4. National Network of the ADA, Information, Guidance, and Training on the Americans with Disabilities Act. https://adata.org/

5. Kurtzleben, Danielle, "House Passes The Equality Act: Here's What It Would Do," *NPR Politics*, February 24, 2021.

6. Bumiller, Elisabeth, "Obama Ends 'Don't Ask, Don't Tell' Policy," *The New York Times*, July 22, 2011.

7. Cooper, Helene, and Shear, Michael D., "Biden Ends Military's Transgender Ban, Part of Broad Discrimination Fight," *The New York Times*, January 25, 2021.

8. Kushner, Howard I. *Retraining Left-Handers And The Aetiology Of Stuttering: The Rise And Fall Of An Intriguing Theory*. 2021.

Chapter 6. Race, Ethnicity, and Cultural Identity

1. U.S. Department of Health and Human Services, *Improving Cultural Competence*, Substance Abuse and Mental Health Services Administration, Treatment Improvement Protocol (TIP) Series No. 59. HHS Publication No. (SMA) 14-4849. Rockville, MD, 2014.

2. Racial and Ethnic Disparities (R.E.D), Department of Youth Services, *Commonwealth of Massachusetts*. https://www.mass.gov/service-details/racial-and-ethnic-disparities-red

3. Morin, Rich, "Exploring Racial Bias Among Biracial and Single-Race Adults: The IAT," *Pew Research Center*, August 19, 2015.

4. deLaszlo, Violet S., editor, *The Basic Writings of C.G. Jung,* The Modern Library, New York.

5. Ibid.

6. Ibid.

7. Greenwald, Anthony, "Psychology data from the Race Implicit Association Test on the Project Implicit Demo website," *Journal of Open Psychology Data,* March 2014.

8. Ibid.

9. Kirshenbaum, Sheril, "A Day To Remember Carl Sagan," *Wired,* May 21, 2011.

10. Robinson, Lena, *Cross-Cultural Child Development for Social Workers, An Introduction,* (Piaget, p. 177), 2020.

11. Ibid.

12. U.S. Department of Health and Human Services, *Improving Cultural Competence,* Substance Abuse and Mental Health Services Administration, Treatment Improvement Protocol (TIP) Series No. 59. HHS Publication No. (SMA) 14-4849. Rockville, MD, 2014.

13. Unruh, Julie, "Sesame Workshop brings magic of Muppets to Middle East after $100M MacArthur Foundation winnings," *WGN9 News,* September 1, 2020.

Beaubien, Jason, "$100 Million Prize Will Deploy Muppets To The Middle East," *Goats and Soda, Stories of life in a Changing World, NPR,* December 20, 2017.

14. Takaki, Ronald, *A Different Mirror, A History of Multicultural America,* 1993.

15. Barajas, Joshua, "Maya Angelou knew how a laugh could be a survival tool," from documentary *Maya Angelou: And Still I Rise,* American Masters, *PBS NewsHour,* Feb 21, 2017.

16. Willett-Wei , Megan, and Lakritz, Talia, "23 eerie photos that show the crumbling beauty of New York's abandoned 'Borscht Belt' resorts," *Business Insider,* July 5, 2018.

17. Kifner, John, "Eldridge Cleaver, Black Panther Who Became G.O.P. Conservative, Is Dead at 62," *The New York Times,* May 2, 1998.

18. Melaku, Tsedale M.; Beeman, Angie; Smith, David G.; and Johnson, W. Brad; "Be a Better Ally," *Harvard Business Review,* November–December 2020.

19. Lattman, Peter, "MLK: Injustice Anywhere is a Threat to Justice Everywhere," *The Wall Street Journal,* January 18, 2008.

20. Gandhi, Mahatma, "Be the change you wish to see in the world."

21. Creary, Stephanie, "How to Be a Better Ally to Your Black Colleagues," *Harvard Business Review*, July 08, 2020.

Chapter 7. Individual and Systemic Inclusions

1. Campos, Jose Edgardo and Root, Hilton L., *The Key to the Asian Miracle, Making Shared Growth Credible*, April 1996.

2. Solorio Alvarez, Angelique, "The Difference Between Diversity and Inclusion and Why It Matters," *ATR International*, December 10, 2020.

3. Rosener, Judy B., "Ways Women Lead," *Harvard Business Review*, November–December 1990.

4. Zukas, H., "The History of the Berkeley Center for Independent Living (CIL)," *Independent Living Institute (ILI)*, 1975.

5. Booker, Brakkton, "MLB Recognizes Negro Leagues As 'Major League' — Correcting A 'Longtime Oversight'," *NPR*, December 16, 2020.

Chapter 8. Systemic Exclusions to Equal Opportunity

Women and Sexism

1. Chozick, Amy, "Hillary Clinton's Beijing Speech on Women Resonates 20 Years Later," *The New York Times*, September 5, 2015.

2. Block, Melissa, "Biden Establishes A Gender Policy Council Within The White House," *NPR Politics*, March 8, 2021.

3. Hernandez, Joe, "The Tomb of the Unknown Soldier had its first all-female guard change in history," *NPR*, October 4, 2021.

Affirmative Action

4. Fuchs, Erin, "JFK wrote a memo in 1961 that still has a huge impact on college admissions in America," *Business Insider*, December 8, 2015.

5. Associated Press, "Affirmative Action Is Backed," *The New York Times*, September 19, 1985

6. Berger, Joseph, "Education; The Bakke Case 10 Years Later: Mixed Results," *The New York Times*, July 13, 1988.

Separate But Equal

7. Hertz, Daniel, "You've probably never heard of one of the worst Supreme Court decisions," *The Washington Post*, July 24, 2014.

History editors, "Thurgood Marshall," *History*, October 29, 2009. https://www.history.com/topics/black-history/thurgood-marshall

8. Levis, Laura, "Putting Social Progress on Par with Prosperity." Harvard Magazine, November-December 2015.

Equal Opportunity in Education

9. Pear, Robert, "In California, Foes of Affirmative Action See a New Day," *The New York Times*, November 7, 1996.

10. Edtorial Board, "Harvard's Legal Discrimination, A federal court upholds the university's race-conscious admissions," *The Wall Street Journal*, October 3, 2019.

Chapter 9. Analytical Tool, *Who versus What?*

1. Eligon, John; Arango, Tim; Dewan, Shaila and Bogel-Burroughs, Nicholas, "Derek Chauvin Verdict Brings a Rare Rebuke of Police Misconduct," *New York Times*, April 20, 2021.

PART FOUR
Post-2020 and Future America

Chapter 10. Government Dysfunction

1. Kristof, Nicholas, "Will We Choose the Right Side of History?" *The New York Times*, October 14, 2020.

2. Gehl, Katherine M. and Porter, Michael E., "Fixing U.S. Politics," *Harvard Business Review*, July-August 2020.

3. "Eliminating the Filibuster," *Indivisible Project*, January 23, 2021. https://indivisible.org/resource/congress-101-filibuster

The National Rifle Association (NRA)

4. Cox Richardson, Heather, *Letters from an American*, March 23, 2021.

5. Ibid.

6. Elinson, Zusha, "Sandy Hook Families Offered $33 Million Settlement by Gun Maker Remington," *The Wall Street Journal*, July 28, 2021.

America's Two-Party System

7. Drutman, Lee, "America Is Now the Divided Republic the Framers Feared," *The Atlantic*, January 2, 2020; author, *Breaking the Two-Party Doom Loop: The Case for Multiparty Democracy in America*.

8. Heim, Phil, "Political history more interesting than fiction," *Faribault Daily News*, July 31, 2021.

9. Rothman, Lily, "Read the First-Ever Republican Party Platform," *Time*, July 18, 2016.

10. Johnson, Lyndon B., *The Civil Rights Act of 1964*, July 2, 1964.

11. Delmont, Matthew, "When Black Voters Exited Left, What African Americans lost by aligning with the Democrats," *The Atlantic*, March 31, 2016.

12. Drutman, Lee, "America Is Now the Divided Republic the Framers

Feared," *The Atlantic*, January 2, 2020; author, *Breaking the Two-Party Doom Loop: The Case for Multiparty Democracy in America.*

13. Ibid.

14. Lepore, Jill, *These Truths, a History of the United States,* 2018.

15. Drutman, Lee, "America Is Now the Divided Republic the Framers Feared," *The Atlantic*, January 2, 2020; author, *Breaking the Two-Party Doom Loop: The Case for Multiparty Democracy in America.*

16. Drutman, Lee, "Why The Two-Party System Is Effing Up U.S. Democracy," *FiveThirtyEight,* June 16, 2021.

17. Ibid.

18. Ingraham Christopher, "How to fix democracy: Move beyond the two-party system, experts say," *Washington Post,* March 1, 2021.

19. Ibid.

20. Ibid.

21. Ibid.

22. Ibid.

23. Ibid.

Chapter 11. A Presidential Election, November 3, 2020

1. Lepore, Jill, *These Truths, a History of the United States,* 2018.

2. Ibid.

3. Ibid.

4. Ibid.

5. Moyers, Bill, "Democracy on the Edge," interview with Steven Harper and Heather Cox Richardson, *Moyers on Democracy,* December 10, 2020.

6. Ritschel, Chelsea, "Ruth Bader Ginsburg Said People Will See This Period In American History As 'An Aberration,'" *The Independent,* September 19, 2020.

7. Silva-Leander, Annika, "The Global State of Democracy 2021, Building Resilience in a Pandemic Era," International Institute for Democracy and Electoral Assistance (International IDEA), October 2021.

A Confederate Flag Flew in our Nation's Capitol on January 6, 2021

8. "It Was an Attempted Coup: The Cline Center's Coup D'état Project Categorizes the January 6, 2021 Assault on the US Capitol," *Cline Center for Advanced Social Research*, University of Illinois Urbana-Champaign, January 27, 2021.

9. Brown, DeNeen L. "Red Summer: When Racist Mobs Ruled, How a pandemic of racial terror led to the 1921 Tulsa Race Massacre," *American Experience*, KQED, February 4, 2021.

10. Lepore, Jill, "A nation born in revolution will forever struggle against chaos...," *These Truths, a History of the United States,* 2018.

11. Obama, Barack, *A Promised Land.*

12. Durr, Sara, "More than 400 Bipartisan Mayors Now Signed on To Letter Calling for Action on Direct Fiscal Assistance for Cities," *The United States Conference of Mayors,* January 29, 2021.

13. H.R.1319, "American Rescue Plan Act of 2021," became law *Congress. Gov*, March 11, 2021.

14. Gale, William G., "Did the 2017 tax cut—the Tax Cuts and Jobs Act— pay for itself?" *Policy, Brookings Institute,* February 14, 2020.

15. Shear, Michael D., "Presidential Speech Highlights: Biden Calls For U.S. to 'Mark Our Independence From This Virus' by 4th of July," *New York Times,* March 11, 2021.

16. Inskeep, Steve, "Why Republicans Are Moving To Fix Elections That Weren't Broken," *NPR Politics,* February 28, 2021.

17. Cox Richardson,Heather, "Anniversary of Bloody Sunday," *Letters from an American,* March 8, 2021.

Chapter 12. Enduring Challenges:
Truth, Misinformation, and Social Media

18. Ortiz-Ospina, Esteban, "The Rise of Social Media," Our World in Data, September 18, 2019.

19. Bryson Taylor, Derrick, "2021 Nobel Prize Winners," *The New York Times,* October 12, 2021.

20. Isaac. Mike and Wakabayashi, Daisuke, "Russian Influence Reached 126 Million Through Facebook Alone," *The New York Times,* October 30, 2017.

21. Gross, Terry and Horwitz, Jeff (author "The Facebook Files," series by The Wall Street Journal), "What Leaked Internal Documents Reveal About The Damage Facebook Has Caused," *NPR Fresh Air,* September 23, 2021.

22. Matt Stieb, "Whistleblower Connects Facebook Decision on Misinformation to Capitol Riot," *New York Magazine Intelligencer,* October 4, 2021.

Black Lives Matter

23. Rahman, Khaleda, "From George Floyd to Breonna Taylor, Remembering the Black People Killed By Police in 2020," *Newsweek,* December 29, 2020.

24. Buchanan, Fessenden, Lai, Park, Parlapiano, Tse, Wallace, Watkins, and Yourish, "What Happened in Ferguson?", New York Times (interactive), updated August 10, 2015. https://www.nytimes.com/interactive/2014/08/13/us/ferguson-missouri-town-under-siege-after-police-shooting.html.

25. Chotiner, Isaac, "A Black Lives Matter Co-Founder Explains Why This Time Is Different," *The New Yorker*, June 3, 2020.

26. Treisman, Rachel, "Minneapolis Reaches $27 Million Settlement With Family Of George Floyd," *NPR*, March 12, 2021.

27. Kirkland, Pamela, "19 Families Buy Nearly 97 Acres Of Land In Georgia To Create A City Safe For Black People," *CNN*, September 12, 2020; "19 Black families purchase 97 acres of land in Georgia, 'Secession,'" *Week Magazine*, Sept. 25, 2020.

28. Blow, Charles, *The Devil You Know,* 2021.

29. Severson, Kim, "Her Family Owned Slaves. How Can She Make Amends?" *The New York Times*, July 4, 2021.

Anti-Asian American Violence

30. "How to Help Stop Hate Crimes Against Asian Americans," *Paper Magazine*, March 17, 2021.

31. Jeung, Russell, Ph.D.; Yellow Horse, Aggie, Ph.D.; Popovic, Tara; and Lim, Richard, "2020-2021 National Report," *Stop AAPI Hate*. https://stopaapihate.org/2020-2021-national-report/

32. Ibid.

33. Wu, Frank H., "Why Vincent Chin Matters," *The New York Times*, June 22, 2012.

34. Grigsby Bates, Karen, "How Vincent Chin's Death Gave Others A Voice," *Code Switch, NPR*, March 27, 2021.

35. Ibid.

36. Jahnke, Art, "Asian Americans and the Model Minority Dilemma, in light of recent attacks, a BU Asian health expert on the group's experiences of racism, alienation, and anxiety," *Boston University Today*, March 23, 2021.

37. Wu, Frank H., "Why Vincent Chin Matters," *The New York Times*, June 22, 2012.

38. Ibid.

39. Little, Becky, "How the 1982 Murder of Vincent Chin Ignited a Push for Asian American Rights," *History Stories*, May 5, 2020.

40. Grigsby Bates, Karen, "How Vincent Chin's Death Gave Others A Voice," *Code Switch, NPR*, March 27, 2021.

41. Grigsby Bates, Karen, "How Vincent Chin's Death Gave Others A Voice," *Code Switch, NPR,* March 27, 2021.

42. Hwang, Roland, "Killing Spawned Asian American Civil Rights Movement, 34th Milestone to Highlight Vincent Chin Case," *Michigan Bar Journal,* May 2009.

43. Grigsby Bates, Karen, "How Vincent Chin's Death Gave Others A Voice," *Code Switch, NPR,* March 27, 2021.

44. Hwang, Roland, "Killing Spawned Asian American Civil Rights Movement, 34th Milestone to Highlight Vincent Chin Case," *Michigan Bar Journal,* May 2009.

45. Grigsby Bates, Karen, "How Vincent Chin's Death Gave Others A Voice," *Code Switch, NPR,* March 27, 2021.

46. Ibid.

47. "How to Help Stop Hate Crimes Against Asian Americans," *Paper Magazine,* March 17, 2021.

48. Biden, Joseph R., Jr., "Memorandum Condemning and Combating Racism, Xenophobia, and Intolerance Against Asian Americans and Pacific Islanders in the United States," *The White House Briefing Room,* January 26, 2021.

49. U.S. Department of Health and Human Services, *Improving Cultural Competence,* Substance Abuse and Mental Health Services Administration, Treatment Improvement Protocol (TIP) Series No. 59. HHS Publication No. (SMA) 14-4849. Rockville, MD, 2014.

50. Davis-Marks, Isis, "Illinois Becomes First State to Mandate Teaching Asian American History," *Smithsonian Magazine,* July 14, 2021.

White Majority, Privilege, and Superiority

51. U.S. Department of Health and Human Services, *Improving Cultural Competence,* Substance Abuse and Mental Health Services Administration, Treatment Improvement Protocol (TIP) Series No. 59. HHS Publication No. (SMA) 14-4849. Rockville, MD, 2014.

52. Cathcart Robbins, Laura, "A White Woman Told Me She Doesn't 'Think Of Me As Black. Here's How I Reacted." *Huffington Post,* September 16, 2021.

53. Newkirk II, Vann R., "The Language of White Supremacy," *The Atlantic,* October 6, 2017.

54. Anderson Cooper interviews Dr. Cornel West, "America as a Failed Experiment," *CNN,* August 28, 2020.

55. May, Payton, "Mancelona parents voice concerns to school regarding white privilege assignment." *MSNBC,* March 11, 2021.

Critical Race Theory

56. George, Janel, "A Lesson on Critical Race Theory," *American Bar Association*, January 11, 2021.

Twenty-First Century Demographics

57. Poston, Dudley L., Jr., "Three ways that the U.S. population will change over the next decade," *Nation, PBS Newshour*, January 2, 2020.

58. Wang, Hansi Lo, "After Months Of Delay, The Census Data For New Voting Maps Is Coming Out August 12," *National, NPR*, August 5, 2021.

59. Cohn, D'Vera, "How accurate will the 2020 U.S. census be? We'll know more soon," *Pew Research Center*, December 14, 2020.

Truth to Power

60. Editorial, "Bayard Rustin: A Gay Man in the Civil Rights Movement," *Black History Month*, April 2, 2021.

61. Cox Richardson, Heather, "Zahid Quraishi, first Muslim American federal judge in U.S. history," *Letters from an American*, June 14, 2021.

62. Halper Evan, "Six takeaways from President Biden's address to Congress," *Los Angeles Times*, April 28, 2021.

63. Ibid.

Conclusion

1. Baldwin, James, *Remember This House.*

2 Peck, Raoul, "James Baldwin Was Right All Along: The writer and activist has the painful, powerful words for this political moment. America just needs to heed them.," The Atlantic, July 3, 2020.

3. Obama, Barack, "Barack Obama Presidential Library Groundbreaking in Chicago," September 28, 2021.

4. Fensterwald, John, "California becomes first state to require ethnic studies in high school,"*EdSource*, October 8, 2021.

Reynolds, Ron, "Ethnic Studies and Private Schools," *California Association of Private School Organizations*, October 13, 2021.

Weissman, Sara, "A Victory for Ethnic Studies," *Inside Higher Ed*, July 21, 2021.

CPSIA information can be obtained
at www.ICGtesting.com
Printed in the USA
JSHW042148060922
30124JS00001B/32